HISTORY

OF

GERMAN LITERATURE

BY

ROBERT WEBBER MOORE
Professor of German in Colgate University

THIRD EDITION

Published for the
BAY VIEW READING CLUB
CENTRAL OFFICE, 165 Boston Boulevard, DETRIOT, MICH.
By the
GERMANIA PRESS
HAMILTON, N. Y.
1903

To My Wife

PREFACE.

THE plan in preparing this work has been to produce an elementary work for those who desire to inform themselves in regard to the great men and the important works of German literature. I have endeavored briefly to show how important epochs have developed, to furnish short biographies of the leaders connected with these epochs, and to present concise outlines of their important works. For the convenience of those unfamiliar with German, I have endeavored to reproduce a large number of titles in English. A large portion of the book, printed eight years ago, and since used as a text-book in eight consecutive college classes, has demonstrated its usefulness in my own work; and in the hope that it may do similar service for others, I have revised and completed it. While numerous and various authorities have constantly been consulted, I wish to acknowledge indebtedness to Scherer's *Geschichte der deutschen Litteratur,* and more especially to König's *Deutsche Litteraturgeschichte* and his *Abriss der deutschen Litteraturgeschichte,* upon which much of the work is based, and from which a portion of the illustrations have been reproduced. Only illustrations of an authentic or historical nature have been admitted.

R. W. MOORE.

Hamilton, N. Y., July, 1903.

SOME PLACES OF LITERARY INTEREST.

BAUERBACH.
Schiller's country retreat after fleeing from Stuttgart.

BERLIN.
Capital of the empire; seat of largest university; Lessing resided there several times at beginning of his career; residence of Spielhagen, Wolff, Sudermann, and many contemporary writers.

BIBERACH.
Residence of Wieland, 1760-69.

BONN.
Residence of Arndt, 1818-60.

BRESLAU.
Residence of Lessing, 1760-64.

BÜCKEBURG.
Herder, court preacher, 1771-76.

COBURG.
Residence of Rückert, 1820-66.

DRESDEN.
Residence of Hauptmann.

DÜSSELDORF.
Birthplace of Heine, 1799.

EISENACH.
Luther a student there, 1498-1501.

EISLEBEN.
Birthplace of Luther, 1483.

ERFURT.
Wieland, professor at University, 1769-72.
Luther a student at the University.

ESCHENBACH.
Residence of Wolfram von Eschenbach.

EUTIN.
Voss, principal of gymnasium, 1782-1802.

FRANKFORT.
Birthplace of Goethe, 1749.

GÖTTINGEN.
University city; many literary men educated there.

GREIFSWALD.
Arndt lectured at the University, 1800-06.

HALLE.
University city, where many literary men were educated.

HAMBURG.
Largest seaport; residence of Klopstock, 1771-1803; residence of Lessing for a few years previous to 1769.

HANOVER.
Birthplace of Schlegel brothers.

HEIDELBERG.
University city where many literary men studied.

JENA.
University city where many literary men studied; Schiller, professor, 1789-91.

KAMENTZ.
Birthplace of Lessing, 1729.

KÖNIGSBERG.
Kant, a professor at the University; Herder, a student at the University; Schenkendorf educated there.

LEIPZIG.
University city; Klopstock, Goethe, Lessing, Richter, and many other literary men were students there; Gottsched and Gellert were professors there.

LORCH.
Schiller's family lived there a short time while he was a child.

LÜBECK.
Birthplace of Geibel, 1815; residence of Geibel, 1869-84.

LUDWIGSBURG.
Residence of Schiller family for a few years after 1766.

MANNHEIM.
Schiller's early dramas first presented there.

MARBACH.
Birthplace of Schiller, 1759.

MAYENCE.
Prominent as home of the Mastersingers.

MOHRUNGEN.
Birthplace of Herder, 1744.

MUNICH.
Capital of Bavaria; Residence of Heyse and many contemporary writers.

NUREMBERG.
Home of Hans Sachs.

POTSDAM.
Lessing wrote *Miss Sara Sampson* there.

QUEDLINBURG.
Birthplace of Klopstock, 1724; Birthplace of Wolff, 1834.

RUDOLSTADT.
Residence of the Lengefeld family.

RÜGEN (Island).
Birthplace of Arndt, 1769.

SÄKKINGEN.
Scene of Scheffel's *Trompeter von Sakkingen.*

SESENHEIM.
Home of Frederike Brion.

STRASSBURG.
University city; Goethe student there, 1770-71. Met Herder there.

STUTTGART.
Schiller educated there; Morike professor there.

TILSIT.
Birthplace of Schenkendorf, 1783.

TÜBINGEN.
University city; Birthplace and residence of Uhland; Kerner, Schwab, and Hauff educated there.

VOLKSTEDT.
Schiller spent the summer there, 1788

THE WARTBURG.
Scene of the Sängerkrieg; Luther spent the winter of 1521-22 there working on his translation of the Bible.

WEIMAR.
Residence of Wieland, 1772-1813; residence of Goethe, 1775-1832; residence of Herder, 1776-1803, residence of Schiller, 1799-1805.

WEINSBERG.
Residence of Kerner.

WETZLAR.
Here Goethe met Charlotte Buff and got the material for Werthers Leiden.

WITTENBERG.
Luther was professor at the University there.

WOLFENBÜTTEL.
Lessing was librarian there, 1769-81.

WORMS.
Scene of part of the Nibelungenlied; Luther brought before the Diet, 1521.

WÜRZBURG.
Burial place of Walter von der Vogelweide.

XANTHEN.
Home of Siegfried of the Nibelungenlied.

CONTENTS.

CONTENTS.

INTRODUCTION.

THE GERMAN LANGUAGE.

The German people form one branch of the Aryan race, many tribes of whom in prehistoric times emigrated from Asia to Europe. Here these tribes, settling in new territories, gradually became separated, and developed into independent nations. Chief among them were Celts, Romans, Greeks, Slavs, and GERMANS.

The various languages spoken by these tribes are called the INDO-EUROPEAN languages, and they are all more or less closely related. According to this relationship the Indo-European languages spoken in Europe are classified into several larger groups,—the Celtic, the Romance, the Slavonic. These groups are further subdivided. For example, to the Romance group belong the Italian, Spanish, Portuguese, and French languages; to the Germanic, the GERMAN, Dutch, English, Danish, Swedish, and Norwegian languages.

History of the language
Each of these languages, whose territory correspons somewhat closely to the political boundaries of the people speaking it, includes several dialects. In German there has been since about 600 a twofold division,—Low German, the broader and softer language of North Germany, and High German, the fuller and harsher language of South Germany; and each of these includes several closely related dialects. High German, which has been the language of most literary productions, has developed through three general periods:—

I. OLD HIGH GERMAN, 600-1100. This was not spoken by the whole German race, but appeared in several dialects.

II. MIDDLE HIGH GERMAN, 1100-1500. This, the lan-

guage of the first great literary period, gradually super-
seded many of the dialects, and became the common literary
language.

III. NEW HIGH GERMAN, 1500-   . This is the written language of Germany to-day. It was created by Luther,
who needed for his translation of the Bible a language that
would be understood all over the country.

PAGAN ANCESTORS OF THE GERMANS

We are indebted for the first detailed account of the
Germans to the Roman historian TACITUS, whose *Germania,*
although written with Roman patriotism as its first motive,
gives a quite reliable account of the people, their country,
their customs, and their religion.   They took great delight
in singing, and on festal occasions songs formed a great
part of the worship of their gods and the celebration of
their heroes; and they were accustomed to enter battle with a
song on their lips.   These songs were their only chronicles
and records.

Their ALPHABET was composed of characters called
RUNES (runa-mystery), which were used for casting lots, for
enchanting, for blessing or cursing, for inscriptions on arms,
drinking-horns, ornaments, etc.   Some authorities believe
that they are of very ancient origin, but recent investigations prove that they are modifications of the Greek and
Roman alphabet.

GERMAN MYTHOLOGY is rich in poetry.   We gain our
knowledge of it from Cæsar, Tacitus, and other sources;
especially from a collection of northern songs called EDDA.
They date from the sixth to the eleventh century.   The manuscript was probably prepared in the thirteenth century, but
it passed out of sight and remained unknown until 1643,
when it was found in Iceland.   In general, it may be said
that the world was ruled by WUOTAN, king of heaven, who
gave comfort and victory to the living, and an immortal

life to the dying. His son DONAR was the red-bearded storm-god, whose brother, the one-armed god of war, bore the name of THIU. His wife FRIJA was the guardian of women. OSTERA was the goddess of the bright morning and of spring. HEL was the goddess of the lower world. In addition to these there existed a whole army of giants and dwarfs, of elves and nymphs.

CHRISTIAN ANCESTORS OF THE GERMANS.

Among the Germanic tribes the GOTHS, who inhabited the lands between the Black Sea and the lower Danube, were the most noble, best endowed, and the most susceptible of development. The gospel was received first by the West Goths, and by them it was carried to several other Germanic tribes, first of all to the East Goths. Their leader was the bishop ULFILAS, whose translation of the Bible is the first important monument in the history of German literature.

Goths converted ULFILAS (311-381) chose the priesthood from earnest conviction. As lector at Constantinople he gained a thorough knowledge of the Scriptures; and when thirty years of age, he was ordained as bishop. For some seven years he preached throughout his native country. Then persecution broke out upon the little church that he had organized, and he with many of his followers fled across the Danube to seek refuge on Roman soil. There the numerous fugitives formed a community that remained under his leadership during the rest of his life, and to which he preached unceasingly and undisturbed. To assure them the gospel, he translated the Bible into the Gothic language. For this translation he adopted an alphabet of twenty-six letters, based on the Runes and the Greek alphabet. He died suddenly at the age of seventy at Constantinople, where he was attending a church council.

The BIBLE OF ULFILAS was honored among his people for centuries, and even in the ninth century it was understood by the West Goths in Spain. Important portions of it have come down to our own times, and they form the foundation for the study of comparative grammar of all Germanic languages. The most complete of these fragments is the *Codex Argenteus* (Silver Manuscript), which since 1669 has belonged to the University of Upsala, in Sweden. It is written with gold and silver letters on purple parchment.

Hero-songs were also common among the Goths, and in them they often mixed history and myth, even celebrating in the same song heroes who had lived centuries apart. The most important of these poems that have come down to us is the HILDEBRANDSLIED, which, when already several centuries old, was written on the blank leaves of a prayer-book by two monks at the monastery at Fulda about 800.

As HILDEBRAND, the vassal of Theodoric, King of the East Goths in Italy, returns to his home after years of exile at the court of Etzel, he is met and forbidden admission to the country by his own son HADUBRAND, whom he had left as a child. Having learned his opponent's name, and realizing their relationship, Hildebrand offers him rich presents if he will desist. The son having heard that his father is dead, insists on the combat. The father utters a heart-rending lament that he should be compelled to fight against his own son. They enter the struggle, cut their shields to pieces — here unfortunately the fragment ends.

Divisions in German literature As the history of German literature has to do almost exclusively with productions written in the High German language, the subject may be divided in the same way as the development of the language—

I. OLD HIGH GERMAN LITERATURE, 600-1100, from the rise of the Franks to the Crusades.

II. MIDDLE HIGH GERMAN LITERATURE, 1100-1500, from the Crusades to the Reformation.

III. NEW HIGH GERMAN LITERATURE, 1500-   , from Luther to the present.

PART I

OLD HIGH GERMAN LITERATURE

600–1100

FROM THE RISE OF THE FRANKS TO THE CRUSADES

CHAPTER I.

EARLY LITERARY MONUMENTS

After the death of Theodoric, the Goths began to decline, and the FRANKS took the lead in German history. They gradually gained control of middle and southern Germany. They accepted Christianity, which at first was a mere outward form, but which by and by came to have a refining and subduing effect on them. The Christianizing influence came from Rome, and was thoroughly Roman Catholic in its nature. Although strict subordination to the Roman Church was unfavorable to literary development, the oldest monuments, *Merseburger Zaubersprüche* and *Wessobrunner Gebet,* as well as many other manuscripts of a somewhat later date, owe their origin to the priests.

Collection of Charlemagne Under CHARLEMAGNE (768-814), who succeeded in uniting both politically and religiously all the tribes of German origin, arose the first prose literature. The Gospel of Matthew was translated, and to this were added baptismal vows and confessions of faith. The great emperor took an active personal interest in cultivating the German language and German literature. He took great pains to have collected and written down the old songs in which the deeds and wars of the old

15

heroes were celebrated. It was his purpose to hand them
down to posterity, but they all disappeared after his death.

Division of the empire
By the time Charlemagne's empire was di-
vided among his three grandsons, the East
Franks were speaking quite a different language
from that of the West Franks. These two sections of the
empire became independent nations, the East Franks under
Louis the German, and the West Franks under Charles the
Bald, and after the treaty of Verdun (843) the term German
Empire is applied only to the Eastern portion. The oldest

Strass-burg oaths
monument of the German language and of the
French language is the oath of agreement
between these two leaders a short time before
the treaty of Verdun. The treaty was made at Strassburg,
and was announced in both German and French.

Two Messianic poems of the ninth century have been
preserved. The first, HELIAND, was written in Low
German about 830. Its purpose was doubtless to make the
Bible known to the Saxons, whom Charlemagne had recently converted to Christianity. The poet tells the Saviour's life according to the Gospels, but in a style entirely
German. The story is Germanized: Christ is represented
as a rich, powerful, yet gentle king; the apostles are the
king's vassals; the Jewish cities are turned into German
strongholds; and all is apparently taking place in Germany.
The best portion is probably that devoted to the Sermon on
the Mount, where Christ, like a German king, surrounded
by his knights and vassals, gives instruction, settles contro-
versies, and decrees justice. The poem closes with Christ's
ascension.

The second, Otfried's EVANGELIENBUCH (Gospels), appeared about 870. Its author was a learned monk of
Weissenburg, the first German poet known by name. The
subject is treated in five books, divided into chapters with
Latin headings. It differs from the *Heliand* in that the

latter is German and popular, while the former is intended to be a learned work throughout, and its purpose was to convert the barbarians to the teaching of the church.

MUSPILLI, another poem of the same period, was probably written on the margins of a book by Louis the German. The author sets forth as well as he can the doctrines of the church, and tries to make them attractive to the nobles. While two armies, angels and devils, are fighting for souls, blood, dropping from the wounded, starts a fire that consumes the world. Hell with its agonies and heaven with its joys are described. Aristocratic sins, like murder, bribery of judges, and quarrels about boundaries, are emphasized.

The LUDWIGSLIED, a historical poem, celebrates the victory of Louis III over the Normans at Saucourt in 881. The king's father dies early, and God becomes the king's tutor. To try him, God sends the Normans to harass his people, and commands Louis to help them. He obeys at once, and entering the battle with a song on his lips, he leads his people to victory.

After the extinction of Charlemagne's line, the SAXONS became the leaders in Germany. Both externally and internally the Saxon emperors raised Germany to a free and independent position. OTTO THE GREAT (936-973) really made Germany the leader of Western Christianity. With the conquering of Italy, came Southern culture; **Roman influence** but with it came also a foreign manner and a foreign language. Although German was the official language, yet in literature, cultivated almost solely by the clergy, Latin was predominant. At the court, in the monasteries and nunneries, the old classics were studied; and the literature of the period, even if treating of native history and legend, appeared in a foreign garb.

WALTHARIUS, a Latin poem written by Ekkehard, a monk

of St. Gall, about 930, is the most important production of this class. Scheffel has used this in his novel *Ekkehard*.

WALTHARIUS OF AQUITANIA, and HILDEGUNDE, daughter of the Burgundian king, have long lived as hostages at the court of Attila. After becoming betrothed they escape, carrying rich booty with them. Attracted by these treasures, the king of the Franks attacks the couple in the Vosges mountains. After a long and serious struggle, there is a reconciliation. Waltharius goes on to his home, marries Hildegunde, and rules his people for some thirty years.

RUODLIEB, another Latin epic of the eleventh century, probably originated in Bavaria, but it has been preserved in fragments only.

RUODLIEB, on leaving his king, whom he has long served, asks for his pay. On being told that he might choose between gold and wisdom, he chooses the latter, and the king gives him twelve rules of conduct, among which were the following : never trust a red-headed person, never pass a church without entering and praying, control anger, postpone revenge at least over night. To these rules, he adds apparently two loaves of bread, one to be opened in his mother's presence, the other on his bridal day. They are, however, vessels of gold and silver.

First poetess In the nunneries, too, Latin was studied, and learned books were written. Foremost among these nuns was ROSWITHA of Gandersheim, a cloister near Brunswick. She early devoted herself to the study of the classics, and frequently imitated Virgil, Ovid, and Terence. She wrote in Latin hexameters a poem in honor of the Virgin, and celebrated the life of Otto the Great in an epic. Finally she ventured into the field of the Latin drama, and composed six comedies in imitation of Terence. She took special delight in representing female martyrdom, and the power and heroic strength which the weaker sex gains through faith. At first her sister nuns were her only audience, but later her works were copied and circulated outside the cloister walls; and one of these copies came to light some five hundred years after her death. She was quite universally admired as the German Muse, and her reputation soon spread over Italy, France, and England.

Volkslied   Among the people, however, the German language still continued to live. In the country and in the cities, was sung what was left of the old hero-songs; many new elements were added to them, and the whole was handed on down to the succeeding generations.

PART II

MIDDLE HIGH GERMAN LITERATURE

1100-1500

FROM THE CRUSADES TO THE REFORMATION

CHAPTER II.

THE GREAT NATIONAL EPICS

The CRUSADES, which during the eleventh and twelfth centuries attracted the gaze of Western nations toward the East, brought new elements of culture to the Germans. The contact with foreign nations, and the renewed acquaintance of the long separated peoples of the West, were beneficial in the development of science and art. Besides the clergy as an influential class, there arose German chivalry, and influenced by French and Flemish knighthood, it attained to more refined manners and higher culture. Rough warfare was changed to a knightly art in the service of God and in veneration of woman; and poetry once more was cultivated in the mother tongue.

In this development of the whole intellectual life, the HOHENSTAUFEN dynasty, especially Friedrich the Red Beard (1152-90) and Friedrich II (1215-50), played a great part.

Swabian dialect Under their influence the Swabian dialect became the language of the court, and since the end of the twelfth century, as pure Middle High German, the leading literary language.

Transition from Old to Middle High German The productions of the twelfth century mark the transition from Old to Middle High German literature and language. Verse and rhyme were far from perfect, but a new element was developing; the subject matter became more varied,

21

and a marked advance appeared in the manner of treatment. The writers were still for the most part monks, but now and then there appeared a poet from among the laity. It was the time of preparation for the splendor of the Middle Ages.

Religious poems
The religious poems of this time are of two general kinds: (1) Those in honor of the Virgin, the most important of which is LEBEN DER MARIA, describing Mary's pious parents, her maidenhood, the birth of the Saviour, and his experiences up to his return from Egypt; (2) those in honor of the church saints. The most important of this class is the ANNOLIED, treating of the life of Archbishop Anno of Cologne (d. 1075). The author is unknown, but he doubtless was some priest living in or near Cologne.

Historical poems
There also appeared numerous historical poems, often a strange mixture of fact and myth. Chief among them is the ROLANDSLIED, a translation of the *Chanson de Roland,* which celebrates Charlemagne and his twelve paladins, who, as protectors of Christianity, are making a campaign against the heathen in Spain. The hero is Roland, of whom little is historically known. He is betrayed and killed in a treacherous manner, but gloriously avenged by the emperor. The poem is filled with the ardent religious feeling that inspired the Crusades, and to this is due its popularity throughout Europe.

Minstrelsy
To this period also belong many poems whose authors are unknown. They were recited at public festivals by wandering poets or minstrels. They were chiefly heroic poems or love poems; some were composed by the minstrels themselves, and some came from various other sources. These minstrels seem to have traveled much; probably they had gone on some of the Crusades and had brought home many poetic ideas from the East. REINHART FUCHS, written by one of these minstrels, is especially inter-

esting because Goethe, some six hundred years later, wove
the same story into his *Reineke Fuchs.*

Hero-songs   In the twelfth century the hero-songs that had
for centuries lived among the people, that had
been recited and handed down orally, began to assume a
more important form.   The authors or compilers who first
put these poems into writing are unknown, and they seem
to have written the poems just as they existed, without add-
ing any of their own personality or their own judgments.
Each of the German tribes or nations had its own particular
cycle of these poems, all of which centered for
Saga-cycles   the most part around the memory of its most
renowned national hero.   The most important of these hero-
songs can, in a general way, be classified as follows:—

The saga-cycle of the lower Rhine, of which SIEGFRIED
of Xanten is the hero.

The Burgundian cycle, whose chief characters are GUN-
THER, HAGEN, and KRIEMHILD.   Their court and home is at
Worms on the Rhine.

The cycle of THEODORIC or Dietrich of Bern, the founder
of the East Gothic kingdom in Italy.   His great vassal is
HILDEBRAND.

The cycle of ETZEL, or Attila, the powerful king of the
Huns. Among his vassals, RÜDIGER is the most renowned.
His home is at Etzelburg on the Danube, probably the mod-
ern Budapest.

The personages appearing in these saga-cycles take a
leading part in the *Nibelungenlied,* which unites these four
cycles in the greatest production of the Middle Ages.

Another cycle, which is the background of the second
important poem of this epoch, is called the *Norman-Saxon.*
The location of the legends is along the coast and on the
islands of the North Sea.   The hero is HETEL, and his
daughter, GUDRUN, is the heroine of the poem named for her.

The first four of these saga-cycles are merged together in the NIBELUNGENLIED, which is composed of thirty-nine cantos, arranged under two heads:—

1. Kriemhild's Love, I-XIX
2. Kriemhild's Revenge, XX-XXXIX

I. KRIEMHILD'S DREAM.—At Worms, on the Rhine, there lived a noble maiden, KRIEMHILD, in company with her mother and her three brothers — GUNTHER, GERNOT, and GISELHER. She dreams that a falcon, which she has reared, is torn to pieces by two eagles. Her mother interprets the falcon to be her future husband, whom she is destined soon to lose.

II-IV. SIEGFRIED'S ARRIVAL.—The renown of the Burgundian king's daughter spreads far and wide through the land. SIEGFRIED, of Xanten on the lower Rhine, hears of her beauty, and with four hundred knights, sets out from his home to woo the maiden. After six days' travel they reach Worms, and ride directly to the castle. HAGEN, Gunther's vassal, is the only one who recognizes Siegfried, and is the only one who can tell of his wonderful deeds: how he had conquered the race of Nibelungs, and had won from them the immeasurable treasure of precious stones and gold; how he had wrung from the dwarf, Alberich, the cloak that makes its wearer invisible; how he had slain the terrible dragon, had bathed in its blood, and thus rendered himself invulnerable. King Gunther and his knights receive the guest with all honor; but a full year passes before Siegfried sees Kriemhild. In the meantime, he helps the Burgundians to conquer the Saxons and the Danes.

V. FIRST MEETING OF SIEGFRIED AND KRIEMHILD.—Finally a feast is prepared in honor of the guest, and the distinguished people of the land are invited. Siegfried and Kriemhild here see each other, and a loving longing seizes them. She thanks him for his service to her brothers, and he graciously replies that it was done to win her favor.

VI, VII. GUNTHER'S WOOING OF BRUNHILD.—Now there lived far away over the sea a beautiful queen of superhuman strength. Whoever wished to woo her was required to surpass the warlike BRUNHILD in three contests,—spear-throwing, stone-throwing, and jumping; whoever was defeated, lost his life.

Gunther had set his heart on this woman, and since he felt his weakness, he betrothed his sister to Siegfried, in return for help in wooing Brunhild. They sail down the Rhine, out into the sea, and after eleven days, reach Isenstein, the castle of Brunhild. Siegfried alone knows the castle and the haughty queen, whom he informs of Gunther's wish.

The contests begin at once. Gunther, unable to cope with Brunhild's superhuman strength, is assisted by Siegfried, made invisible by his magic cloak. As the Burgundian king comes out victorious, the queen Brunhild is compelled to yield. She, however, refuses to follow him to Worms until she has sent word to her friends and vassals.

VIII, IX. SIEGFRIED'S JOURNEYS. — The Burgundians are annoyed at Brunhild's delay, and to avoid any danger, Siegfried secretly sails to the land of the Nibelungs, where his treasure is still concealed; here he chooses a thousand of his best knights, and returns to Isenstein, where Gunther announces that they are his men. Brunhild arranges the government of her country and goes with Gunther to the Rhine.

X. THE DOUBLE WEDDING.—The two couples are married at the same time, yet over the happy marriage feast threatening clouds are gathering. Fierce, jealous envy fills the heart of Brunhild, when she beholds Siegfried at the side of Kriemhild; and in the night her uncontrollable war-passion returns; she struggles with her husband, overcomes him, binds his hands and feet, and hangs him up on the wall, where he remains until morning. When, on the following day, he and Siegfried are alone, the latter promises to help him subdue his bride. Concealed in his magic cloak, he enters Brunhild's apartment, and after a long struggle, overcomes her. On leaving, he carries her girdle and a gold ring which he has taken from her finger. Later he gives to Kriemhild these two articles, which are to bring destruction to her whole race.

XI. SIEGFRIED'S RETURN HOME.—Shortly after the wedding festivities, Siegfried and his bride return to the Netherlands, where his father gives him control over land and people. For ten years peace and happiness reign in both courts.

XII, XIII. SIEGFRIED'S JOURNEY TO THE COURT BANQUET. —During this time Brunhild seeks to conceal her jealousy under the oft-renewed pretext that Siegfried is neglecting his feudal service. Gunther in vain tries to quiet her. Then she pretends to be desirous of seeing Kriemhild. Gunther finally invites them to a feast. The ceremonies are carried on in a magnificent manner; the contests last for ten days, when they are interrupted by a tone of discord.

XIV. The Quarrel of the Queens.—On the eleventh day, Kriemhild and Brunhild together watch the knightly contests and recall bygone days. In these recollections, Kriemhild gives vent to the emotions of her heart, and says to Brunhild: "My spouse is such a knight that all these lands and kingdoms ought to obey his might." Brunhild angrily replies that that would be impossible, because Siegfried is Gunther's vassal. The trouble breaks out afresh, when the two queens meet at the church door, and Brunhild says: "Stand still; before the queen shall never proceed the vassal's wife."

Kriemhild, greatly excited, betrays the secret of the bridal night, and shows, in proof of her statement, the ring and girdle that Siegfried had given her. Brunhild, deeply offended, begs her husband to take vengeance on the perpetrator of this shame. Gunther and Siegfried try in vain to quiet the matter. Hagen, seeing Brunhild's tears, promises the revenge she desires, and even influences Gunther to assent to the plans for Siegfried's murder.

XV. Hagen's Treachery.—Hagen learns from the unsuspecting Kriemhild the location of the one vulnerable spot on Siegfried's body,—yes, even induces her to indicate that spot by sewing a little cross on her husband's coat. A great hunting party is organized and Siegfried invited.

XVI. The Murder of Siegfried.—At her husband's departure Kreimhild is heavy-hearted. He, however, enters heartily into the chase, and even joins Hagen and Gunther in a race to a spring. He reaches it ahead of the others, but politely waits for Gunther to drink first. As he bends over to drink, Hagen seizes Siegfried's spear, and thrusts it through the spot marked by the cross. Siegfried dies with a heart-rending prayer to the murderers in behalf of his wife.

XVII-XIX. Kriemhild's Complaint.—On the following morning, Kriemhild finds her husband's corpse before her door, whither Hagen had caused it to be carried. The body is removed to the church, where the murderer is soon made known by the wounds bleeding afresh at Hagen's approach. After her husband's burial, Kriemhild visits his grave daily; no one is able to console her. For over three years she sees neither Gunther nor Hagen, but finally becomes reconciled to her brother, and consents to the removal of the Nibelung Treasure, her dowry, from Siegfried's former home to Worms. She gradually forgets her grief in the joy of giving bountifully to all around her. Hagen, fearing the great influence she might have by her giving, sinks the treasure in the Rhine, where, according to popular tradition, it still remains. (When the Burgundians gained possession of this great treasure, they took the name Nibelungs, and had to endure the terrible curse that accompanied it.)

For thirteen years Kriemhild mourns Siegfried's death, and is on the point of withdrawing to a convent, when news comes from over the Rhine that changes her mind.

XX-XXII. ETZEL'S WOOING AND WEDDING.—After the death of his wife, ETZEL turns his thoughts toward Kriemhild, and sends Rüdiger to woo her for him. Kriemhild hesitates long, but when Rüdiger takes a solemn oath to avenge any wrong done to her, she consents to marry Etzel. With a stately escort, Kriemhild starts eastward, and is met by Etzel and his train not far from Vienna, whither they repair to celebrate the marriage. Amidst popular rejoicing in honor of the newly married couple, festivities, whose splendor and magnificence had never before been equaled, are carried on through seventeen days. On the eighteenth, they ride out of Vienna, embark upon the Danube, and sail to Etzelburg (Budapest), where the festivities are renewed. Yet in all this glory and homage, Kriemhild can scarcely conceal her tears at the memory of Siegfried.

XXIII-XXX. JOURNEY OF THE BURGUNDIANS TO ETZEL'S COURT.—Thirteen years later, after she had borne a son, and honor and love had been bestowed upon her by both king and people, Kriemhild still finds herself a stranger, and can not overcome her grief at the loss of Siegfried and her desire for revenge. Finally she influences her husband to invite to a feast her brothers and friends, who, notwithstanding Hagen's emphatic disapproval, accept the invitation, and splendidly equipped start eastward, reaching the Danube without misfortune. There a mermaid warns them that, except the chaplain, none of them should ever return home. Hagen, in his anger, pitches overboard the chaplain, who swims safely to shore,—a proof of the truthfulness of the warning. Hagen destroys the boat that had carried them over, and they proceed on their way with heavy hearts. Before they reach Etzel's court, they are warned of Kriemhild's attitude. She rejoices at their coming, as she imagines the day of her revenge near at hand. After an interchange of harsh words between her and Hagen, she forbids the Burgundians to carry arms,—a command that Hagen refuses to obey.

HAGEN and VOLKER unite in acting as leaders of the Burgundians; and their stalwart forms and bold demeanor make such an impression on the Huns, whom Kriemhild had urged to take vengeance on Hagen, that not one of them dares to enter combat with them.

XXXI-XXXVI. IN THE CATHEDRAL.—On the following morning, the princes, heavily armed, go to the church to commend their souls to God. When Etzel, surprised at their armor, asks if anyone has offended them, Hagen cleverly replies that the Burgundian princes carry arms for three days at all court festivities. While the princes and leaders were being royally entertained at a banquet given by King Etzel, his brother, BLÖDE-LIN, at Kriemhild's instigation, falls upon and kills the Burgundian vassals, who were dining in another hall.

When the news of this calamity reaches the chiefs, Hagen begins the work of revenge. He strikes the head from Etzel's and Kriemhild's child, and then he and Volker go marching up and down the hall, striking blow after blow with their swords. After Gunther in vain tries to stop the horrible struggle, he and his brothers join in the work of revenge. The king and queen make their escape, and Rüdiger, who had treated the Burgundians kindly on their journey, is given permission to withdraw with his five hundred men. All the rest are put to death. But new Huns keep coming, and the contest rages until evening. At last the Burgundians seek reconciliation; but as they can obtain it only by giving up Hagen, they refuse to accept it. The raging queen has the heroes driven into the large hall, and orders it set on fire. All night long the brave men stand there amidst the falling timbers, protecting themselves with their shields, and drinking blood to quench their thirst. Six hundred of them live through this ordeal, and bid their enemies defiance.

XXXVII, XXXVIII. RÜDIGER'S DEATH. — Rüdiger, although greatly excited, has thus far remained neutral. His heart is inclined toward both parties. Kriemhild reminds him of the oath he took when he came to woo her for Etzel, and Etzel reminds him of his duty as vassal. Both call on him for help, and after a hard struggle, his duty as vassal leads him to renounce his friendship to the Burgundians, whom he and his subjects now assail. He and all his people, however, are slain. Next, the Gothic knights, without Dietrich's consent, and under the leadership of HILDEBRAND, enter the contest. A struggle rages between them and the Nibelungs, from which only Hildebrand on the one side and Gunther and Hagen on the other, escape with their lives.

XXXIX. THE END OF THE NIBELUNGS.—When Dietrich of Bern hears this, he goes to the two Burgundians, assuring them of their lives and safe return home, if they will become his hostages. When they refuse, he conquers Hagen first, and then Gunther. Both are bound and taken before the queen, and then imprisoned separately. Kriemhild, who had agreed to spare the lives of both the heroes, first addresses herself to Hagen, promising to forgive him all, if he will restore to her the Nibelung treasure. When he declares that he has sworn never to reveal its resting place as long as one of his lords is living, she has her brother's head cut off, and carries it herself to Hagen, who now refuses to tell her where the treasure lies. She at once strikes off his head. Old Hildebrand, unable to endure such a sight, springs upon the woman and puts her to death.

> "The royal feast was ended in sorrow and in pain;
> As joy draws ever sorrow behind it in its train."

Subject matter of the epic The subject matter of the epic is much older than its present form, which dates from the first part of the thirteenth century. It is based on two general sources,—mythological characters and the tales belonging to very remote, prehistoric periods, and historical persons and events from the time of the Migrations, as they are described in the early hero songs.

Historical elements Chief among these are GUNTHER (d. 437), who, with a large portion of his people, was killed in a battle with the Huns, which in reality was fought west of the Rhine, but the legend transfers it to Etzel's court; ETZEL, or Attila (d. 453), the great king of the Huns, called "the scourge of God;" and THEODORIC (d. 526), whose long and peaceful reign over the Goths in Italy began twenty-five years after Etzel's death, but the poem represents him as Etzel's vassal. The mythical element is seen in the name of the poem, which means, "inhabitants of the dark realm of mist," and in the characters of the dwarf and mermaids, and Siegfried and Brunhild. These characters in earlier form appear in the *Edda,* where Siegfried, called Sigurd awakens Brunhild from her sleep within a circle of fire, liberates her, marries her, and then deserts her. This, no doubt, is the real explanation of her mortal hatred toward him in the later poem, where it seems to arise from jealousy toward Kriemhild. In the Edda the legend appears ruder in form and more savage in character than in the *Nibelungenlied.* Into the interweaving of the historical and mythical elements, there has come the influence of Christianity and Chivalry, giving the harsh and passionate characters of the earlier legend gentler and more refined qualities.

Mythical elements

Christianity and Chivalry

History of the poem The poem was known and loved among the people until the sixteenth century. With the seventeenth it seems forgotten. About the middle of the eighteenth, Professor *Bodmer,* of Zurich, found at Hohenems in Switzerland two bulky manuscripts, which proved to be the *Nibelungenlied.* From that time until to-day, it has been subjected to careful study; has been translated several times into modern German, and into all modern tongues. Besides the two manuscripts found by Bodmer, eight other complete and some eighteen incomplete ones have come to light.   The *Nibelungenlied* has become a household book; it is read and studied in the higher schools; editions with historical or mythological commentaries are numerous; the story has several times been worked up into more modern literature; and artists have found it a rich source for study.

Authorship   The authorship of the poem is a disputed question; some maintaining that it is a loose collection of popular songs strung together, others that it is originally the work of a single poet. The truth probably lies between the two; namely, some poet of good taste and judgment has taken the various songs as he has heard them, and reproduced them in the spirit of the times. He is not the author of the legends, but the author of the poem as it now stands; yet his name, as well as the home of the poem, is unknown.

GUDRUNLIED, the second national epic, embodies the legends of the North Sea. Already known at the beginning of the twelfth century, it was worked over into its present form about 1210, by some now unknown poet. Probably he was from the South, and traveling northward, found these legends, which he transferred to parchment. At any rate, the poem has to do with the North and with the races to which our forefathers belonged. In it we may see the traits and characteristics of our ancestors in their home by the sea, with its storms, its ships, and its sea-kings. Much there is in it that is barbarous and harsh, yet, amidst it all, many things beautiful and admirable appear. The influence of other poets can be traced, and we can see that the author was acquainted with the *Nibelungenlied*.

Description of Gudrunlied

Comparison with Nibelungenlied   Comparing the two, we may say that the *Nibelungenlied* is more warlike and tragic. The *Gudrunlied* is somewhat softer in character; the leading figures are women; domestic life is made prominent; and there is much wandering to and fro. The latter may be called a gratifying contrast to the former. While Kriemhild's desire for revenge destroys a great and noble race, Gudrun's magnanimity is a strong power in leading two hostile races to reconciliation. If Kriemhild's fidelity is repulsive on account of her degeneration, this womanly virtue in Gudrun makes a pleasing impression.

Preservation   The poem is handed down in a single manuscript which, prepared at the order of Emperor Maximilian I (1493-1519), was found at the castle of Ambras in the Tyrol, just 300 years after Maximilian's death. It is now in Vienna. Like the *Nibelungenlied,* various editions and numerous translations of it have been published.

The poem, composed of thirty-two cantos, called adventures, is divided into three sections, of which the first two serve as an introduction to the third.

I.

HAGEN OF IRELAND (I-IV).—HAGEN, son of Siegebant, of Ireland (a place in Holland), is carried off by a griffin and left on an island, where he, in the company of three royal maidens, who had been carried away like himself, grew to manhood. Having learned to use the weapons which he had taken from the corpse of a shipwrecked sailor, he slays the griffin, and later hails a passing ship, which takes him and his three companions home. He marries the most beautiful one, HILDE.

II.

ABDUCTION OF HILDE (V-VIII).—When Hagen's daughter, also called HILDE, has grown to maidenhood, he is unwilling to give her to any suitor who is not stronger than himself. King HETEL, of Hegelingen (probably Friesland in Holland), sends several heroes, relatives, and vassals of his, among whom are FRUTE of Denmark, HORANT the singer, and WATE the knight, in a magnificent ship to Ireland. There they pretend that they are merchants, banished by King Hetel, and they are cordially received. Horant's music delights Hagen's court, and especially Hilde, to whom is made known their real mission, and who allows herself to be carried away. Hagen pursues the abductors; he overtakes them at their landing place, where, in a fierce contest, both Hagen and Hetel are wounded. At last, however, they are reconciled, and Hetel marries Hilde, with her father's best wishes.

III.

1. GUDRUN'S ABDUCTION (IX-XIX).—Hetel and Hilde have two children,—a son, ORTWIN, and a daughter, GUDRUN, who surpasses her mother in beauty. She is wooed and courted by kings and princes, but her father will give her to none of them. Among these rejected suitors are SIEGFRIED, of Moorland; HARTMUT, of Normandy; and HERWIG, of Seeland; all of whom are determined to gain their bride by force. Herwig first returns with an army, and by noble actions, wins the heart of his loved one. She steps between him and her father as they fight, makes peace between them, and is betrothed at once to Herwig. When Siegfried hears this, he marches against the fortunate suitor, to whom Hetel now hastens with help. While Hetel and his knights are away, the third suitor, HARTMUT, carries off Gudrun and sixty-three other maidens. When Hetel and Herwig are informed of this, they make peace with Siegfried, and all start in pursuit. At Wülpensand, an island near the mouth of the River Scheldt, a battle takes place, in which Hetel is killed, and his army defeated. During the night the Normans gain their ships and escape with their prize. At the break of day, the Hegelings realize that their number is too small to pursue the enemy, and they return home to wait for another generation to grow up.

2. GUDRUN'S CAPTIVITY (XX-XXVII).—For thirteen years Gudrun remains in custody of Hartmut, who at first treats her kindly, hoping to gain her love. Not succeeding, he yields to his mother's request, and turns Gudrun over to her. She is compelled to build fires, and wash the clothes on the seacoast. This treatment is no more effectual than Hartmut's kindness; Gudrun remains faithful to her betrothed. In her native land, the boys have grown to manhood; an army is equipped; and one day, when Gudrun and one of her companions are washing clothes, they are met by Herwig, her betrothed, and Ortwin, her brother, who had come as spies. Recognizing her, Herwig wishes to take her at once, but her brother objects, because he never will steal

from the enemy what had been taken from him by force of arms. Promising to take her from the castle the following day, they go back to sea. Joyfully Gudrun returns, pretending that she is willing to marry Hartmut. This brings her kind treatment.

3. GUDRUN'S RESCUE (XXVIII-XXXII).—Early next morning the Hegelings storm the castle. Hartmut's father and mother are killed, Hartmut himself is taken prisoner, but at Gudrun's request, is pardoned. After their return home, there is a quadruple wedding: Ortrun, Hartmut's sister, who had been a true friend to Gudrun, is united with Ortwin, and Hartmut is wedded to Hildburg, Gudrun's companion, when washing clothes, on the same day that Herwig and Gudrun are married. Siegfried marries Herwig's sister.

CHAPTER III.

COURT EPICS AND THE MINNESONG

Character
Court epics are quite different from the national epics. They are the product of chivalry, dealing not with matters of national importance, but with court etiquette and social decorum. They treat not of native popular lore, but abound in foreign traditions. The common people are not heard of, and the universe seems to be an opportunity for fashionable sport and sentimental love-making. There is little background to them, and they are visionary. The writers are of noble rank, and their works are filled with peculiar and wonderful adventures, which are frequently interspersed with moral discussions. Four men have been specially successful in this kind of poetry,—HEINRICH VON VELDEKE, WOLFRAM VON ESCHENBACH, GOTTFRIED VON STRASSBURG, and HARTMAN VON AUE.

HEINRICH VON VELDEKE, the "father of court poetry," was the first man to apply to verse strict measurement and exact rhyme, and he was the first prominent representative of the court epic. He came from a family of knights in the Netherlands, but of his early life almost nothing is known. Later we find him as a poet at the court of Cleve. Here he had written over ten thousand verses of his *Eneit* (1184), when the manuscript was stolen from him. After nine years of searching, he found it in Thuringia, and here he remained quite a while at work.

The Eneit
The poem is based on Virgil's *Æneid,* but the heroic deeds are treated very briefly, while the love scenes are carried out to great length. A few verses suffice to describe the destruction of Troy, and the flight of the hero to Carthage, but two thousand verses are necessary to depict Dido's love for Æneas. The latter goes to Italy,

and is kindly received by Latinus, who is ready to give him his daughter; but her mother prefers Turnus. In reply to her mother's question as to her love for Turnus, Lavinia shows that she knows nothing of the nature of love. This leads to a long digression in which the mother tries to instruct her daughter in the nature of love. But to no avail; for love remains a secret until Æneas appears. Then she understands the secret, for "Venus shot a sharp arrow that wounded her heart so that she was compelled to love whether she would or not." Lavina discloses her love to Æneas, who joyfully fights with Turnus, and is victorious.

WOLFRAM VON ESCHENBACH, the greatest German poet of the Middle Ages, was a Bavarian, and takes his name from the town of Eschenbach, where he was born between 1170 and 1175. He was trained in all that pertained to the calling of a knight, but could neither read nor write. In his travels he had learned enough French to enable him to understand French poems, when read to him; and his quick mind gained him a treasure of general knowledge. The most of his life was spent on his estate near Eschenbach, but he passed a few years at the Wartburg, where HERMANN OF THURINGIA gathered around him the best poets of the age. Here it was that about 1207, according to tradition, he took part in the Sängerkrieg (poets' contest). While here he composed many short poems, and also *Parzival*. After Hermann's death (1210), he returned to Eschenbach, where he died about 1220.

In PARZIVAL two saga-cycles are united: (1) The Legend of KING ARTHUR; (2) The Legend of the HOLY GRAIL. To understand *Parzival,* we must first consider briefly these two sources, which, originating partly in Wales and Brittany, and partly in Northern Spain and Southern France, were expanded by French poets into great poems. From these French productions, the German writers of court epics all took much of their material.

KING ARTHUR, the center of the British legend, was the leader of the Celts in Wales against the invading Anglo-Saxons, and was murdered by his nephew, probably in the sixth century. This is about all that is known of him, yet among his people he was regarded as the model of knight-hood. Gradually he assumed in the minds of the people the form of an ideal knight and king, surrounded by thousands of heroes, who spent their time in the service of women. His court is situated on the Usk, in Wales. From the large numbers, King Arthur chose twelve, who composed the "Round Table," so called from the fact that they sat at a round table where none could think himself more favored than the others. To belong to this circle was the highest honor that a knight could ever attain.

From the court the knights set out in quest of adventures, —to relieve the oppressed, especially ladies; to conquer giants and traitors. These cavaliers were models of refinement and politeness, and the ladies of the court excelled in grace and beauty.

The HOLY GRAIL legend is quite different, and was prob-ably used by the clergy to counteract the worldly legends of Arthur. The word "Grail" means a vessel or cup, from which the Lord, on the night when he was betrayed, gave food to his disciples, and in which Joseph of Arimathæa caught the blood from the crucified Saviour. Since that time the Grail possessed the power of giving eternal life, and protected those who in faith looked upon it. Angels kept this treasure until TITUREL built a castle upon Mount Salv-age, in northern Spain, where it was kept by spiritual knights of the Grail. Strong manhood and bravery, faithfulness to God and to woman, self-sacrifice and humility, were the requirements for admission to this order. To the Grail Castle no one could come who was not called; and, on the other hand, the secret of the Grail was made known only to him who asked. Whoever gained the secret needed to trouble himself no more about earthly things; the Grail provided food and drink. To be received into this knighthood was the highest attainable good to which man might aspire.

Besides these two elements, a third is worked into the poem,—that of the EVIL SPIRIT, working ruin and destruction. While the knights of the Grail spend their energy for the glory of God, and the cavaliers of Arthur follow their ambition for renown, and seek joy in the company of ladies, the Evil Spirit is planning destruction for both spiritual and worldly chivalry.

These are the principal sources from which Wolfram took the material for *Parzival*. These he has worked up in a manner that is original and entirely his own. It is a psychological poem; not merely a romance to delight the fancy by its numerous incidents, but it deals with questions that have always occupied men's minds. "Parzival is a representative of the sinful man, who, trusting to his own powers, despairs of God and himself, and obtains the heavenly kingdom only by repentance and humility."

PARZIVAL is born soon after his father's death, and his mother, HERZELOIDE, retires to a forest to shield him from all knowledge of chivalry, which had led to his father's death. Scarcely has he grown to manhood, when a chance meeting with some of King Arthur's knights leads him to ARTHUR. His mother, having clad him in fool's clothing, that ridicule might drive him back to her, and having given him much advice, consents to the separation, at which she dies of a broken heart. After many adventures, he arrives at King Arthur's court, and arouses commotion by his peculiar costume. Yet he soon wins esteem by killing a knight and donning his armor. An old knight teaches him everything becoming in a man of his rank, and advises him not to ask many questions. He rides out into the world, and comes to a city, whose queen, CONDWIRAMUR, he frees from oppression, and afterward marries. A longing for home and mother, whose death is unknown to him, drives him away. He goes to the Grail Castle. His uncle, King

ANFORTAS, unknown to him, is sick; but mindful of his instruction, he asks no questions, even about the beautiful and wonderful things around him. He does not imagine that the recovery of the lord of the castle and his own happiness depend on his asking the cause of sickness and sadness there. Had he asked that question, he would have been made lord of the castle. Then, with a heavy heart he leaves. Just as he is received into the Round Table and has attained the highest honors, CUNDRIE, the messenger of the Grail, appears and overwhelms him with maledictions, because at the sight of so many wonders on Mount Salvage, he had not asked the question. With sad glances they all look at him, as he leaves the Round Table, and, at enmity with God and man, he rides away once more to seek the Holy Grail.

PARZIVAL wanders for five years. One day he meets a company of pilgrims, led by a gray-haired knight, who talks earnestly to him, and sets him to thinking. Wishing to learn more, he follows the man, whom he finds to be his uncle, and from whom he learns about the Grail and about his mother's death. Better still he learns to believe in God's goodness and mercy, and to bow his will to God's will. Reconciled with God, and forgiven of his sins, he leaves his uncle. To serve God is now his only ambition, and he finally reaches such spiritual purification that he is declared worthy to become lord of the Grail. As king he enters the castle of the Holy Grail; frees Anfortas from suffering, by asking the once-neglected question, and by a prayer before the Grail; is united once more with his wife and two sons, of whom the older, LOHENGRIN, is to be his successor as lord of the Grail.

GOTTFRIED VON STRASSBURG, of whom very little is known, flourished at the close of the twelfth and the beginning of the thirteenth century. The material for his best work, *Tristan und Isolt,* was drawn from French sources, and it abounds in French expressions. While Wolfram delighted to depict high ideals and morals, Gottfried went to the opposite extreme, and described luxuries and even wanton life.

TRISTAN, celebrated for heroic deeds, is sent by his uncle, MARKE, to woo for him the beautiful ISOLT. With considerable misgiving, she follows the suitor homeward; but on the way they both fall madly in love with each other, under the influence of a love potion intended for the king, which they had unintentionally drunk. The king is frequently warned of their love, but he will believe nothing about their guilt. When at last his eyes are opened, Tristan escapes. In a strange country he falls in love with another Isolt, although he can not forget his former love. Here the poem breaks off. It has been completed in one way or another by several poets. A pleasing continuation is in Tennyson's *Last Tournament,* in the *Idyls of the King.*

HARTMANN VON AUE, a Swabian by birth, and a contemporary of Gottfried, attended a cloister school in his youth, and became so well versed in Latin and French as to be able to call himself learned. Among his contemporaries he was regarded as the master of court poetry, and was noted for his moderation. His style is clear, and his verse moves along with pleasing purity. His material is drawn largely from Latin and French sources. Two of his poems, *Erec* (much resembled by Tennyson's *Enid*) and *Iwein,* are named after Knights of the Round Table, and they, becoming popular, added much to the glory of Arthur.

Der arme Heinrich is his best production.

HEINRICH, a Swabian knight, forgetful of his duty toward God, is punished with leprosy. After seeking help in vain, he learns from a great physician that he can be restored if a maiden will voluntarily give her life-blood for him. The daughter of one of his tenants, hearing of this, offers herself, and goes with the leper to the physician. At the decisive moment, realizing what he is doing, he prevents the girl's death. Now that his mind is clear, God relieves him from his physical disease, and he marries the maiden who was ready to sacrice herself for him.

Alongside of the few authors of court epics, there arose a number of writers of lyric poetry. To this class of writing, existing in various forms and treating of numerous subjects, the common name MINNESONG is given. The term "minne" has several meanings, the oldest and best being that of kind remembrance or love of a friend. In the best of the songs the term is used in this sense; but later it attained a licentious meaning, to which many of the poems correspond. In honor and in service of women, these songs of the court poets were sung; they told of love's sorrows and joys. The love of nature, especially the return of spring, permeated all the poems. The praise of women culminates in the glorification of the Virgin Mary. The noblest of the Minnesingers paid homage to the Christian religion, and sang in the service of God. Many of the wandering minstrels extolled the royal patrons from whom they received their support.

Of the numerous manuscript collections of these poems that have come down to us, the most important is the LARGE HEIDELBERG MANUSCRIPT. This remarkable book, containing the songs of one hundred and forty poets from the twelfth to the fourteenth century, is a magnificent folio, bound in red leather, and adorned with the French royal coat of arms embossed in gold. It contains 429 leaves of strong parchment, upon which the songs are written in a beautiful, uniform, and legible hand. The first letter of each stanza is painted in bright colors, and nearly every poet is represented by a picture. Each poet appears in a characteristic position or action. The first two are royal Minnesingers. After these come the poets of higher and lower nobility, who in turn are followed by those from the people. The pictures are not authentic portraits, but they present us ideas from the life of chivalry: pictures of war, of domestic scenes, pictures of love incidents, and of many interests of chivalrous life. Walter von der Vogelweide is sitting on a stone, wrapt in thought. Wolfram von Eschenbach stands in full armor, at the side of his horse, ready to mount.

History of the Manuscript By whom the manuscript was prepared, and where it was first kept, is unknown. Toward the end of the sixteenth century, it was found carefully preserved at a castle in the valley of the upper Rhine. In 1607, it was purchased for the library in Heidelberg. During the Thirty Years' War, in some unknown manner, it was taken to Paris, where for two centuries, under the title of *Paris Manuscript,* it formed one of the treasures of the National Library. In 1888, thanks to the emperors William I and Frederick III, it was restored to the library in Heidelberg, and is now called the *Large Heidelberg Manuscript.*

WALTER VON DER VOGELWEIDE, the greatest of the Minnesingers, was born in the Tyrol between 1165 and 1170, and was from a family of the lower nobility. In Austria he learned the art of poetry, and composed his youthful minnesongs, and later became a wandering minstrel, and tried his fortune in political songs, now with one party, and now with another. Although he often changed parties, his patriotism and his praise of the German land and of the German women were ever the same. He traveled over Germany, and even in France and Hungary, singing his songs. Resting from his wanderings, he tarried a while at the court of Hermann of Thuringia, where he took part in the Sängerkrieg. In many a poem he praised his patrons, but never descended to common flattery. Whenever he thought it right, he raised his voice against the emperor and princes just as freely as against the pope and the priests. Although he had traveled far and wide, he had nowhere found a home, and not one of the many princes who petted him, gave him a fixed dwelling-place.

The emperor at length gave him a small fief, probably near Würzburg. There he passed the following years in quiet seclusion. Whether he followed his patron on a crusade or not, is unknown; but at any rate he has given proof of his interest in the movement and his love for the Holy Land.

Subjects of his poems Although he sang of many subjects, the larger portion of the poems are love songs. In his old age he tells us: "Fully forty years have I sung of love." His minnesongs were pure and sweet, full of praise of woman and her gentler qualities. Among his spiritual songs, the one addressed to the Trinity is the best. Of his last years and of his death (1230?) we know nothing. But we do know that he was buried in the cathedral at Würzburg. A legend relates that, in his will, he provided the means for feeding and watering daily the birds at his tomb. He had four cups cut into the stone which he wished to cover his grave; and into these the grain and water were to be put.[1]

---

[1] Cf. Longfellow's *Walter von der Vogelweide.*

CHAPTER IV.

DECADENCE OF MIDDLE HIGH GERMAN LITERATURE.

1300-1500.

Civil troubles — Even in the thirteenth century, the decline of literature had begun, and the two following centuries completed the decadence. The emperor and the princes paid no attention to literature and art, but were fighting among themselves for their own aggrandizement. The lower nobles sank down to the level of the robber-knight, and plundered the merchants as they passed to and fro. Among the clergy things were no **The clergy** better. Immorality and ignorance went hand in hand. Even at the celebrated monastery of St. Gall, the abbott and the monks were unable to write their names. Intellectual life was rekindled by the newly founded universities, and through them prose received a great impetus; but poetry was cultivated only among the masses of the people, and the folksong is the only really poetical production of this period.

In the fourteenth century, the poetical inheritance which for two centuries had been cherished by the knight, passed into the hands of the middle class. From the minnesong there arose the MASTERSONG, and the cultivators of the latter took delight in tracing the origin of their art back to the Minnesingers. The mastersong was cultivated in societies or guilds, into which the artisans of the cities organized themselves, that they might cultivate music and poetry. Mayence is regarded as the first city in which this art was cultivated; but in most of the important cities of southern Germany, the mastersong flourished. These singing societies were carefully organized, and everything in connection with them was carried on in accordance with established rules.

According to the *Tabulature,* an established collection of laws, regulations, fines, and penalties, the art of writing the mastersong had to be learned from a recognized master; and after the pupil had spent some time as an apprentice, he was subjected to an examination before a session of the singing school. Here he had to demonstrate his knowledge of the science of rhyme and meter, and also his skill in handling them. If the examination was satisfactory, the candidate was received as a member of the guild; but he became a master only after he had composed some original tune.

Frequently these worthy masters met informally in the inns; but their principal gatherings took place in the church on Sunday. An excellent description of one of the Sunday sessions is to be found in Hagen's novel, *Norica,* a brief extract of which follows:—

The interior of the church was beautifully decorated, and the society of mastersingers presented a festal appearance as they sat there, some of them with long gray beards, and some, smooth-faced youths, all of whom, however, were as still and as earnest as if they had belonged to the seven wise men of Greece. A bautiful show they made, in their rich, silk garments of green, red, and black. Near the pulpit stood the singer's rostrum, much like a pulpit. In the forward part of the church a small platform was erected, upon which stood a table and a desk. Here were stationed the judges who were to keep track of mistakes, either in form, contrary to the tabulature, or in subject matter, contrary to the Bible. The first singer was the gray-haired CONRAD NIGHTINGALE, a locksmith, who uttered many a beautiful and accurately rhymed stanza about the heavenly Jerusalem. The judges were busy, one reading the Bible, another counting the syllables on his fingers, and the third writing what the other two now and then whispered to him.

The masters in the audience were busy; their fingers kept up an effort to follow the measure; and the shaking of their heads indicated a mistake. The second master was young FRITZ KOTHNER, a bell-founder, who had chosen the story of creation as the subject of his poem. The poor fellow was embarrassed, and could not proceed. In disgrace and confusion he left the floor. A worthy old man clad in black, LEONARD NUNNENBECK, took his place, and carried the audience through his poem about the Lord and the majesty of his heavenly abode. The fourth was MICHEL BEHAIM, a weaver who had seen many lands. Carefully had he practiced, for this was his first appearance. When he had finished, the judges left their seats; one went to Nunnenbeck, and hung around his neck a chain with a picture of King David attached. The second adorned Behaim's head with a garland of silk flowers. These were not gifts, but merely tokens of honor for that day.

Subject matter

As we see from this description, the art of these masters was dedicated principally to sacred subjects. King David was their model, and they strove to write as he wrote. Sometimes their materials were of a lyric nature, but their idea was that poetry was always mechanical, and not the embodiment of free inspiration. Although the mastersong reached its height in the sixteenth century, it flourished in the seventeenth, and existed even in the eighteenth. It was cultivated in most German cities, but its great center was at Nuremberg, where HANS SACHS lived.

Value

The mastersong must not be judged by what it accomplished in the singing school, for many of the writers pushed out and produced their best works in forms forbidden by the rules. Finally a national and a religious meaning must be attached to the work. When the artisan, during his leisure hours and on Sunday, contemplated the history of his people, the glory of their emperors, the gradually developed power and beauty of his native city, he was strengthened in his patriotism. The dealing with Biblical subjects led to the careful consideration of faith in God and in the church. The Bible, open on the judge's desk, led to independent thinking, because it led to the comparison of the Bible doctrines with the practices of the church. Thus some preparation for the work of the Reformation was made.

Of more poetical importance is the FOLKSONG, which, existing in a modest way from the earliest times, in the fourteenth and fifteenth centuries, came to remarkable development. It is different from the mastersong, in that it is always fresh and natural, true to life, and untrammeled. The author is generally unknown. It goes from lip to lip, from race to race, and from century to century. It is always sung, never declaimed. Text and tune are inseparable. In the streets, in the inns, in the towns, and in the forests it

Subjects is sung by joyous people. It treats of various subjects, prominent among which are drinking, traveling, dancing, the cradle, soldier life, student life, and devotion to fatherland. Many of these old folksongs are still the most popular of German student songs, and large numbers of them are known through their English translations.[1]

Didactic poems The degeneracy of the times, especially the roughness of the nobility and the corruption in the church, had long been calling for energetic reform. This found a poetic expression in numerous didactic poems, largely satirical in nature. The most important of these is the *Narrenschiff* (1494), by Sebastian Brant (1458-1521), who lived most of his life at Strassburg, where he was long an important officer of the city.

A ship chosen by the author as the only conveyance large enough to carry all the fools to Narragonia (Fool-land); and when the horn is blown for departure, a motley crowd of madmen, from all classes of society, come hurrying on board; they rush over the gangway; they clamber over the sides of the ship; they fairly fight for early place on the list. All told, they number 113 — fops, misers, dotards, drunkards, voluptuaries, bigots; everyone gets a ticket and a fool's cap. Each division of the

---

[1] Cf. Longfellow's *Beware.*

poem describes some particular kind of fool and all are aptly illustrated by woodcuts, for which the drawings were made by Brant, who humorously puts himself at the beginning as a book-fool. The journey of this mad crew to Fool-land is described in rhymed verse, but with little rhythm and less elegance, yet all the way through pointed and droll.

Drama
1. Religious
Although the beginnings of the drama are to be found among the earliest Teutons, its real development came with the representations by the clergy at the great church festivals, as Easter and Christmas. The Saviour's birth and suffering and Old Testament history formed the material to be brought before the people. These were first written in Latin, and were called plays (ludi). They were performed in the churches, and there gradually arose a series of passion plays, Easter plays, and Christmas plays. But even as early as the fourteenth century there became woven into them a comic and ludicrous element, which led to their being shut out of the churches here and there. Then (about 1300) they were carried to the open market-place, where the rudest sort of stage served for the representations. The language was changed to German, and laymen presented them. They frequently lasted several days, and a common order was as follows: On the first day, the suffering and death of the Saviour; on the second, his descent into hell; on the third, his resurrection and ascension. The windows, doors, and roofs of the houses around the market-place served as auditorium. As scenery was unknown, various localities were represented side by side,—e. g., heaven, hell, the manger at Jerusalem, and the city itself,—and the actors went from one place to another right before the audience. Toward the end of the Middle Ages the whole life of the Saviour was represented, also many of the Old Testament stories that pointed to Christ.

2. Secular
During the fifteenth century, the comic element that had been increasing for some time came to an independent dramatic development, and alongside of the

religious there arose the secular drama; alongside of the tragedy, the comedy, or as it was called at that time, *Fastnachtspiel,* which was played on the last night before Lent. This new play consisted largely of processions of young people clad in all sorts of masquerading, and they were accompanied on all sides by tricks and jests, vulgar, and often immoral in their nature.

From a Painting by O. Brausewetter

MARTIN LUTHER

HANS SACHS

PART III

NEW HIGH GERMAN LITERATURE

FROM THE REFORMATION TO THE PRESENT TIME

CHAPTER V.

ERA OF THE REFORMATION.

With the opening of the sixteenth century, there came
a new era. The discovery of America, the estab-
**Revolution
in thought** lishment of universities, the revival of interest
in classic antiquity, and the invention of printing,
had brought about a complete revolution in thought. All
this had its influence on language and literature. But more
than this was the life and influence of one man. MARTIN
LUTHER appeared, and with him began, not only for the
church, but also for German literature, for German language,
for German science, for German poetry, a new era.

Martin Luther was born Nov. 10, 1483, at Eisleben, and
after receiving his earlier education at Mansfeld, Magdeburg, and also at Eisenach, where he spent three years in
the Cloister School, he entered the University at Erfurt in
1501. At first he began the study of law, but soon turned
his attention to theology, and four years later entered the
monastery. In 1508, he was called to the University of
Wittenberg, where he lectured on the Scriptures, and where,
in 1512, he gained his doctor's degree. In 1517 he nailed to
the church door in Wittenberg his ninety-five theses opposing
the sale of indulgences by Tetzel. From this time on, open
war raged between him and the pope; and when
**Excommuni-
cation** the latter, in 1520, excommunicated him, Luther
publicly burned the papal bull. Called to Worms,
he declared his personal faith in Christ and his Word, and

refused to recant, as the pope had demanded. He was then

At the Wartburg
pronounced an outlaw, but found a refuge with Frederick the Wise, at the Wartburg. Here he began, about Christmas, 1521, the task of translating the Bible. When he left the Wartburg the following March, the most of the New Testament was ready; but not until 1534 did the whole work appear. The rest of his life he spent in restless activity, devoted to the development of the reformation in church, school, and home. He died in 1546 in his native town, Eisleben, and was buried in the church at Wittenberg.

Luther's Bible
Luther's greatest service to German literature was his translation of the Bible, by means of which he became the reformer of the German language, as well as of the German church. In the latter part of the fifteenth century, there developed in the imperial courts and in the cities a language different from the numerous dialects, which was gradually becoming a bond between the North and South. Luther himself tells us that he chose no particular dialect, but used a language familiar to all. It was the language of the Saxon court, which the princes and kings of Germany spoke.

New High German
To have freed this language from dialect, and to have made it the common High German literary language, is Luther's greatest service to literature. Especially through his translation of the Bible, which came into the people's hands all through Germany, did this new High German gain a foothold, and become the exclusive literary language that has remained until the present time.

His originals
His was the first translation that was not made from the Latin version of the old church. He took the originals, the Hebrew and the Greek, and transferred their thought accurately into the thought and the language of his people. He revised his work again

and again, until his last edition was published in 1545. Well may we say, in the words of one of Germany's greatest philologists: "Never has any other book in the world been so well translated as Luther's Bible."

Other writings Besides this, he wrote numerous prose works, all of which are models of clear and forcible style. Among the most important are Bible interpretation, sermons, catechisms, controversial writings, letters, and table talks. His oratory, too, was the best of his time. His addresses were always great, often irresistible. His whole soul, with all its warmth and fire, was in his speech, and he affected high and low alike. The German evangelical hymn, also, is due to Luther, who **Hymns** was a lover of music from his childhood. Before the Reformation, German song was seldom heard in the churches; but Luther encouraged and cultivated it in every possible manner, and brought it to its great popular honor. Thirty-seven hymns are attributed to him, written in the plain language of the masses, and filled with Biblical truth. Many of them are adaptations of Latin hymns. Only eight are entirely original, and among these his Christmas hymns are the best. Seven are free arrangements of the psalms, among which is his greatest and best, "A mighty fortress is our God," the one that has been the Protestant battle song in trial.

Among the people of no other language has the church hymn had so strong a hold on the masses. To appreciate its influence, one must hear a German congregation sing. One element that made these hymns so popular during the Reformation, and which makes them so to-day, is that they were created, not for the people, but right out of their life and thought, and in their own words. Only ideas familiar to them all, and only experiences common to them all, are sung. Furthermore they are, for the most part, written in forms which had been familiar for centuries, and often the melody is borrowed in whole or in part from the old secular songs. It was an easy thing for the artisan to keep the new religious ideas in mind, by singing them as he worked. The servant sang as she washed her dishes, the farmer sang as he plowed, and the mother sang at the side of the cradle.

Luther and the Reformation were aided by HANS SACHS, who was born at Nuremberg[1] in 1494. At the Latin school he laid the foundation for his education, and at fifteen, he began the shoemaker's trade, being instructed at the same time in the art of the mastersong. For five years he traveled through Germany, visiting various singing schools, that he might perfect himself in poetry; and while traveling, he composed his first original poem. Returning to his native city, he settled down as a shoemaker. Although he worked at his trade industriously, he gained a wide acquaintance with literature, and developed a remarkable poetical activity. Six thousand and forty-eight poems came from his pen.

His position in literature He was the best known and most popular poet of the sixteenth century. He brought the mastersong to perfection, and was the pride of the Nuremberg school. But his four thousand mastersongs have not brought his name to posterity. They do not rise far above the products of the singing schools; and he himself thought so little of them that he did not admit them to his published works; they were intended merely to adorn and maintain the singing school. His **Most lasting work.** most lasting work is in his sayings, or proverbs, which gradually appeared in print.

In praise of Luther and his teaching, which he knew thoroughly, he wrote many poems. In *Die Wittenbergisch Nachtigall* (Wittenberg Nightingale) he compares the pope with a lion, the bishops and priests with wolves, the monks and nuns with serpents; but Luther is called the nightingale that, with her pure singing, drowns the howling of the wild

---

[1]Cf. Longfellow's *Nuremberg*.

Hymns

animals. His hymns, although earnest and full of warmth, are by no means equal to those of Luther. Yet they are tender, musical, and spontaneous. In the drama, too, he has done real service. By his spiritual plays he has helped his people better to understand the Bible, from which he chose his material.

Drama

By his stiff and dry tragedies, for which he chose his material from classical antiquity and from French romances, and from the stories and legends of the Germans, he extended the historical view of his people, even if he did not succeed in putting into new dramatic form any idea of the past. As a dramatist, he is best in his comedies and farces.

Greatest among his contemporaries, he was entirely forgotten by succeeding generations, until Goethe brought him into favor. Now he stands as one of the noblest figures among the companions of Luther.

One of the most prominent representatives of the epic, didactic, and satirical poetry of the sixteenth century is JOHANN FISCHART (1540?-90), who after studying at different universities, settled as a lawyer at Strassberg, where, however, he devoted more attention to literature than to law. As a warm friend of the Reformation, he devoted his literary activity to furthering this cause. He attacked the Jesuits vigorously, and worked in a positive way by writing hymns, improving the catechism, praising music, and using it to the honor of God. Deep piety and intellectual gifts appear in his shorter poems. In the *philosophisch Ehezucht-büchlein* (Marriage-book) he depicts the joy and peace of home life; and in the *Anmanung zu christlicher Kinderzucht* (Christian Education) he treats of parental duties and childhood joys. His *Glückhaft Schiff von Zürich* (Luck Ship) describes the journey of a party of Zurich riflemen, who in one day brought their boat down the Rhine to Strassburg. His greatest work is a satiric novel, based on *Gargantua et Pantagruel* of Rabelais.

**Volks-
bücher**

Prose writing came more and more into favor, and many a French book was worked over and popularized in Germany. Much more worthy of attention are a number of genuine German stories and farces, which even to-day are known as VOLKSBÜCHER. The most important of these are the *Faustbuch, Der ewige Jude,* and *Till Eulenspiegel.*

The FAUSTBUCH, contained the history of the famous magician, Dr. Faust. A man by this name undoubtedly did live and gain great renown. He was a chemist and a magician. At Erfurt he summoned Homer's heroes before the students. On account of his antics and his enchantments he frequently came into danger of being arrested, but always escaped with such quickness and ease that people began to believe he had the power of becoming invisible. Finally he was found one morning dead in his room. After that, the story became more and more mysterious; everything fantastic, ghostly, and devilish attached itself to the name of Faust. The legend was first committed to writing by an unknown author and published at Frankfort in 1587. According to this old *Faustbuch,* Faust had entered into a compact with the Devil, in order to satisfy his thirst for knowledge and to enjoy life to the fullest extent. After he had passed over all Europe with his companion, reveled in every pleasure, and by the most wonderful actions had astonished the whole world, he was taken away one night by the Devil, in accordance with the compact they had made. MARLOWE dramatized the story from a version which had been printed in London, and later GOETHE made it the framework of his great masterpiece.

About the year 1547 a student in Hamburg is said to have met DEN EWIGEN JUDEN (The Wandering Jew), and to have learned his story. This tall, old, shabbily dressed man claimed to have lived in Jerusalem at the time of Christ, and when the Saviour, burdened with the cross, wished to stop and rest before his door, he drove him away. Then Christ said to him: "Because thou hast denied the Son of man rest, no rest shall henceforth be allotted thee. Thou shalt continue to wander until I come again." The curse was fulfilled, and for fifteen hundred years he had been roaming aimlessly about the world, unable to live in peace and unable to die. His experiences during these hundreds of years form the substance of a *Vilksbuch,* which appeared in 1602, without the name of the author. This, like so many of the other Volksbücher, has furnished material to many a recent writer.

TILL EULENSPIEGEL is the title given to a lot of jokes and pranks that tradition has attached to a person who is supposed to have really existed, and to have been called Till. The rest of the name, "Eulenspiegel," is derived from the old proverb: "Man recognizes his own faults just as little as an ape or an owl, who, looking into a mirror, recognizes his own ugliness." The oldest extant edition of this book, containing sage speeches, practical jokes, pranks, etc., of the laboring class, appeared at Strassburg in 1515.

Alongside of these stories the VOLKSLIED continued to flourish, and the themes were extended by the introduction of historical and political songs. Yet at this time, as in the previous generations, the most popular of these songs were short and of a lyrical nature. Love with its woes and joys was by far the most common theme, but the subjects were still as numerous as they had been during the centuries before, and the people of every class and of every occupation had their own appropriate songs. Gradually, however, a new and strange element entered, which served to take these songs away from the masses—the songs were gathered into books, and while studying the new and artistic arrangement of the music, the people forgot the words; learned expressions and even mythological references crept in; and finally foreign adornment, an effort to copy the poetic forms of the South, completely destroyed the simplicity and naturalness of the folksong. Thus it happened that in the seventeenth and eighteenth centuries the folksong fell into disrepute, and was regarded as somewhat common and vulgar, until HERDER, GOETHE, BÜRGER, UHLAND, and HEINE brought it back into favor.

CHAPTER VI.

PERIOD OF THE THIRTY YEARS' WAR AND THE SEVENTEENTH CENTURY.

Revival of learning
Following Luther's work in the Reformation, there arose promise of great revival of learning and culture in Germany. The school system was remodeled; biography was cultivated; translations from the classics were undertaken; tales and proverbs became popular; secular songs were added to the religious ones; and romances met with much favor.

Besides the beginnings in these lines, there was activity in the line of the drama, which, however, was interrupted just at its most hopeful stage. All the hopes cherished with regard to the drama and all other literary activity were completely wrecked by the bursting of the storm that had long been gathering, the THIRTY YEARS' WAR (1618-48). This fatal scourge was begun as a war between Protestants and Catholics; a war which, for thirty years, shook Germany, and tore her to pieces; which devastated and depopulated her mercilessly; which even threatened to destroy her. From a war of religions it became a war of peoples.

Nature of the War
On German soil fought people of foreign nations, some as allies of one of the contesting parties, but more as pirates eager to take advantage of the civil discord for the furtherance of their own selfish ends. Danes and Swedes, Frenchmen, Spaniards, Italians, devastated Germany and promoted the destruction of her native Protestant and Catholic princes. Town after town disappeared in flame;

Condition of the country
the unarmed people were tortured and killed with brutal ferocity. From the war with its attendant famine and disease, Germany lost wellnigh half of her population; and the other half was left in poverty and despair. Her national spirit was broken; she

lay in a prostration from which generation after generation
has been necessary to revive her. In their weakness the
princes of Germany cast their eyes across the
Admiration for France Rhine, and, imagining that everything great and
royal was embodied in Louis XIV, they imitated
slavishly the court of Versailles. Customs, morals, language,
and literature soon passed under the curse of the worst side
of the French influence. French became the language of the
court and of society.

To this must be added that in the pulpits a dry
Church and universities and spiritless orthodoxy, instead of the life-giv-
ing gospel, was preached.   In the universities,
the teachers were little better. Alongside of
profligacy among the students, there reigned in the lecture-
hall talks a dry and lifeless formality which added its weight
to all the other influences that were sapping the national
life. As French was the language of the courts and of society, so in the educational circles Latin became the prevalent
language.

Under all these circumstances, it is evident to
Foreign influence everyone, no literature could be produced. And
when, after the country began to recuperate from
the effects of the war, some new impulse began to appear,
it was so closely modeled after the French, Italian, Spanish,
English, or Latin that almost a whole century passed before
the German literary world awoke to realize that it must
change its tactics and become national.

Notwithstanding these discouraging circumstances strong
efforts were made to cultivate the German language and to
bring German poetry to a place of honor; but these efforts
were all of a somewhat scholarly character, and sometimes
ran into very peculiar channels. Thus arose the SPRACH-
GESELLSCHAFTEN (Language Societies), which had for their
purpose the purifying of the language by removing all foreign words and dialectic expressions. Among the most im-

portant of these were: (1) *Die Fruchtbringende Gesellschaft,* founded at Weimar in 1617; (2) *Die Teutschgesinnte Genossenschaft,* founded at Hamburg in 1643; (3) *Der Gekrönte Blumenorden,* founded in Nuremberg in 1644. In general we may say that these societies were composed of princes, nobles, and scholars, thus rightly pointing out the democratic basis as the only one on which German literature could prosper.

Independent of these societies there flourished several poets who were generally regarded as leaders, about whom there gathered various schools. The first of these was MARTIN OPITZ (1597-1639), a native of Silesia. While still a student in the gymnasium he wrote a treatise *Ueber die Verachtung der deutschen Sprache* (contempt for German) in which he enjoined the educated classes to cultivate German poetry and the German language. After preparing for the profession of law, he traveled in the Netherlands, and became infatuated with the stiff Dutch poetry. His life was an unsteady one; wherever he went, his aim seemed to be to gain the favor of the princes by his literary art.

Service to literature Among his contemporaries his writings passed for those of a great genius, but they are simply smooth and skillful verses, without inspiration or real life, and furthermore, many of them are merely translations from the French and the Dutch. Yet he soon became a model whom most of the literary men imitated. His services to literature are purely of a formal type, and in his *Buch der deutschen Poeterey* (German Poetry) he succeeded in establishing new laws of versification. He pointed out the difference between classic and German rhythm, showed how accent should take the place of quantity, and maintained that an accented syllable should be equivalent to a long one, and that unaccented ones should be considered short. He introduced the French Alexandrine, which held almost complete sway in German poetry until the time of Klopstock and Lessing. He insisted on the use of pure German words, and urged writers to avoid all dialectic expressions.

Opitz's followers

The followers of Opitz are generally grouped under the title of *The First Silesian School,* and among them the first to be mentioned is PAUL FLEMING (1609-40), who while a medical student at Leipzig gained considerable skill in writing poetry for student gatherings. On the completion of his student days he was sent on an embassy to Russia, won his medical degree at Leyden, and died at Hamburg at the age of thirty-one. He far surpassed Opitz in natural endowments, and may be regarded as the foremost lyric writer of his time. Many of his spiritual songs have lived even to our day. Other members of this school were ANDREAS GRYPHIUS (1616-64), whose melancholy disposition and almost continued illness saddened his character and his writings; and FRIEDRICH VON LOGAU (1604-55), whose short, pointed epigrams contrast agreeably with the tiresome circumlocutions of most of the members of this school. The best work of Gryphius is in his dramas. The tragedies abound in the horrible and the terrifying, but his comedies are full of good humor and wit. Logau patriotically complains of the sad conditions of the fatherland, but never loses hope for happier times in the future.

PAUL GERHARDT (1607-76), after Luther, the greatest hymn-writer of Germany, became the leader of a number of poets, largely clergymen, who have contributed numerous songs to the *Liederschatz* of the Protestant church. Gerhardt, educated at Wittenberg, was pastor of one of the Berlin churches, but his strict Lutheran ideas would not harmonize with the Calvinistic tendencies then cultivated by the government, and he finally had to give up his post. His numerous hymns are always fresh and full of piety. The church festivals, Advent, Christmas, Easter, are especially represented in them. They are written in a high and cheerful spirit, and at once became popular. Many of, them have found their way into our American hymn-books. Among this latter class may be mentioned: " O sacred heart, now wounded," "Give to the winds thy fears," "Since Jesus is my friend," and "Here can I finally rest." He wrote several patriotic songs, and from an artistic standpoint, he may be regarded as one of the greatest lyric writers of Germany.

Second Silesian School   The dry formalism of the First Silesian School gradually led to a reaction, which went hand in hand with the political disintegration of Germany, and with the introduction of French laxity. The Silesian poets coming to the front during the sixties are grouped under the title of the Second Silesian School, and they endeavored to introduce sweetness of style and gallantry of expression into their writings, but this so often led to sickly sentimentality and inflated expression that the term "Bombastic" is frequently applied to the period. Like the preceding school, they believed that the poetic faculty could be acquired; and therefore the ability to write poetry was regarded as a part of every cultured man's education.

Leaders of the Second Silesian School   The leaders were HOFFMANNSWALDAU (1618-79), whose pure and honorable life contrasted markedly with the rough and profligate style of his love poems; and LOHENSTEIN (1635-83), who imitated Hoffmannswaldau in his lyric poems. In his dramas, however, he chose Gryphius as his model, and even surpassed him in piling up the horrible, the unnatural, and the vulgar. While most of the material for his dramas is taken from Roman or Turkish history, for his best work, a prose romance, *Arminius,* he chose a home subject, and in it gives with wearisome details the whole history of the

Germans, and endeavors to show that everything great was due to them.

Opposition to the school

The errors of this school could not fail to produce opposition. Earnest men arose and endeavored to lead poetry back to simplicity and truth, but in their endeavors they went to the other extreme, that of cold and formal versifying. In this movement the lead was taken by CHRISTIAN WEISE (1642-1708), who introduced into his gymnasium the art of making verses, so that his pupils might learn to use their tongues. He was a prolific writer, having composed something like a hundred dramas, many of which were acted by his pupils as drill in poetic art. Among these his comedies are the best. His novel *Die drei ärgsten Erznarren in der ganzen Welt* (The Three Biggest Fools in the World) gives a forcible picture of the manners of the time, and is still worthy of being read. Two other men of this class were GÜNTHER (1695-1723), whose bright promise of a glorious career was cut off by his wild and dissolute life; and BROCKES (1680-1747), a great worshiper of nature, but without any creative genius.

Romance

In the romance of this century the foreign element predominated. French, Italian, and Spanish stories of love and chivalry were worked over into German. They were made didactic. It was regarded as part of their mission to educate and improve morals, and into these love stories whole text-books of the most varied kinds—history, geography, astrology, etc.—were woven. The Thirty Years' War brought abundant material for quite a different kind of romance—the romance of adventure. The best production of this kind is *Der Abenteuerliche Simplicius Simplicissimus,* at once the best German romance of the seventeenth century and also one of the best of all times. Its author was CHRISTOFFEL VON GRIMMELSHAUSEN (1625-76), a native of Hesse, who was reared among soldier surroundings, and later wandered over Germany, France, and Switzerland.

Into his *Simplicissimus* he has undoubtedly woven much from his own adventurous experience, and to this is largely due the freshness that prevails in the book.

The hero of this story—the son of a gentleman—grows up in absolute neglect in the home of a peasant whom he regards as his father. When this peasant is maltreated by the plundering soldiers, SIMPLICISSIMUS flees into a forest, where he finds a refuge with a hermit who proves to be his own father, and who now gives him the attention he has long lacked. After two years his father dies, and the poor boy is carried off by soldiers to be a page to the governor of Hannau. He soon becomes accustomed to the rough manners of the soldiers, and although his conscience strives against it, he sinks lower and lower in the scale of sin. As a soldier he is noted for his bravery and dexterity, and he is very successful in his search for booty. As a prisoner he is carried off to Sweden, then comes to Paris, and leads a regular robber-life until he is so disgusted with it that he settles down, marries a peasant girl, and manages a farm. This proves a failure, his wife dies, and once more he takes up his wandering, going this time to Asia, and returning only after the war is over. He now learns of his real parentage, repents of his sins, and withdraws from the world to end his days as a hermit.

The appearance of Defoe's *Robinson Crusoe* (1719) aroused interest throughout Europe. It was translated into German within two years, and had such a run that in a short time nearly every trade and province had its own Robinson. The most important story of this kind was *Insel Felsenburg* by GOTTFRIED SCHNABEL, which describes in four large volumes the experiences and fate of a Saxon who, with three other persons, escapes from shipwreck to an island, where he marries one of his companions.

5

Satire   Satire went hand in hand with romance, and often borrowed its guise. MOSCHEROSCH (1601-69) wrote a satirical romance under the title of *Wunderliche und wahrhaftige Gesichte Philanders von Sittenwald* (Wonderful and True Visions of Philander of Sittenwald), which, although not free from many of the faults he ridicules, gives a very good picture of the times, and is at the same time a pious and patriotic work. BALTHASAR SCHUPP (1610-61), pastor at Hamburg, was a powerful preacher and writer, and his works are models of simplicity. Those that are known to us are of a satirical nature, and are directed against the immorality of the times. ABRAHAM A SANTA CLARA (1644-1709) is another whose efforts in the same line gained him renown. He was court chaplain at Vienna. His greatest work is *Judas der Erzschelm* (Judas, the Arrant Knave), and from one of his sermons Schiller borrowed part of the Capuchin's sermon in *Wallensteins Lager*.

CHAPTER VII

THE FORERUNNERS OF THE CLASSICAL PERIOD.

The Middle of the Eighteenth Century

The seventeenth century closed with foreign influence still resting on Germany, which had by no means recovered from the Thirty Years' War. Gradually there arose among literary men the idea that poetry consists in the imitation of nature. Firmly established in this belief were three men; two of them professors in Zurich, the other a professor in Leipzig. The discussion as to how this principle should be carried out soon led to the LEIPZIG-SWISS CONTEST, in which the Swiss, soon supported by an ever-increasing number of influential Germans, won the victory and prepared the way for a new period, which was to become the richest that Germany has, as yet, known.

In 1720 the two Swiss professors, BODMER (1698-1783) and BREITINGER (1701-76), organized a poets' society, the aim of which was to exchange ideas and opinions about literary questions, and to criticise one another's productions. The members soon established a periodical, *Die Discurse der Malern*, in which they might publish their ideas about painting. They regarded poetry as an art, which paints with words, like painting; therefore they called themselves painters, and signed their articles with the names of renowned artists. According to their philosophy, poetry must flow spontaneously from the heart and mind, and must be carried on by lively fancy. As models they chose the English in preference to the French. BODMER's importance lay in his comprehension of the real nature of poetry. From his boyhood he was attracted to English literature, and he translated Milton's *Paradise Lost*. He has, furthermore, done great service in publishing, and thus bringing to the world the treasures of the Middle Ages, the *Nibelungenlied, Parzival,* and the poems of the Minnesingers. He was a lover of poetry and of poets; and he delighted to receive into his home the young poet's of his time. Klopstock and Wieland, in their young manhood, found a home with him, and in his old age he welcomed Goethe.

In opposition to the principles of the Swiss society a strong influence was exerted by the Leipzig professor, GOTTSCHED (1700-66), who thus far had reigned supreme as a teacher and critic of German literature. He believed the essence of poetry to be in the imitation of nature, yet he thought this imitation should be hemmed in by reason and regularity, and should be restricted to predetermined forms. As models he chose the French poets of the time of Louis XIV (Corneille, Racine, and Molière), who alone "had rightly comprehended the spirit of classic antiquity." The contest between him and his distant opponents became more and more animated until a passionate war of words was hotly waged on both sides; the climax came in 1740, when he turned his scorn on Klopstock's poetry. This led to his defeat, after which he never regained his former influence.

His service to literature   Yet Gottsched has done good service to literature. The German language, which he strove to free from foreign words, was brought through his influence into the higher social circles; and through his periodicals he was enabled to arouse interest in German literature. His influence was felt in the theater, too, whence he banished the popular but for the most part impure pieces, although he produced nothing better to take their place. He had no place for Shakespeare, but translated several dramas from Corneille and Racine. His own dramas, written in imitation of the French, are of little importance. He was assisted in his literary work by his wife, a lady of fine education and distinguished talents, in many respects intellectually superior to her husband.

Reaction against Leipzig poets
In 1744 many of the Leipzig poets broke away from the influence of Gottsched, and founded a new periodical, the *Bremer Beiträge*. The most influential among these was CHRISTIAN GELLERT (1715-69), who, restrained by his bashfulness from entering the ministry, chose teaching as his profession, and was soon appointed professor of philosophy and ethics at the University in Leipzig. Although his delivery was very poor, he soon attracted large numbers of students.

His influence
His influence extended far beyond the lecture room; in both Protestant and Catholic circles he was respected, and his counsel was sought on all kinds of subjects. Peasant and prince loved him, and Frederick the Great regarded him as the most rational and reasonable of the German professors. He possessed none of the gifts of a poet; creative power, lofty fancy, and depth and fullness of thought were wanting. Yet the best of his work still lives fresh among the German people of to-day.

Fables
His fables still delight both young and old; and many of his spiritual songs still comfort and console sad and hesitating souls. His feeble attempts in the drama have very justly passed into oblivion.

In Halle, about 1739, a second important poets' club arose, whose leaders were three students, GLEIM, GÖTZ, and Uz. Their ideal was Anacreon, the Greek poet of wine and love, at the court of Polykrates, about 530 B. C. Named for him, they were called ANACREONTICS, and sang of happy, careless enjoyment of life, under the protection of Venus and Cupid, and in honor of their ladies, to whom they gave Greek names, as Delia and Chloe. A higher idea of life came into their poetry through their admiration for Frederick the Great, whose heroic deeds had aroused the slumbering national feeling.

The most important man of the group was JOHANN

WILHELM GLEIM (1719-1803), who passed the most of his life as canon at Halberstadt. He enjoyed a good income, and his home was a hospitable resort of literary men. Goethe says, "His great delight was to help young men in literary activity." Through his kindness he has done more for the development of literature than he did by his own writings.

Among those who felt his influence may be mentioned KLOPSTOCK, WIELAND, LESSING, and others who found welcome and encouragement in his attractive home. He was not a great genius, but he could adapt and criticise in a way that was helpful to those around him. All through his life he was a strong patriot, and was able to encourage the young authors about him to maintain and develop the national side of their literature. Most of his poetry has passed from notice, but that in which the national element predominates, especially *Preussische Kriegslieder von einem Grenadier* (Prussian War Songs by a Grenadier), in which he glorified the great Prussian king, is still known and appreciated.

Service of these men to literature   Among these men of the early part of the eighteenth century, there was not one of great and original genius. Imitation was their forte, and although they were apt in their imitating, French influences are everywhere prevalent. They are overshadowed and almost forgotten, but great honor is due them as the forerunners in a great intellectual revival. They did not attain to great development, yet they took a paralyzed literature, gave it some new life, and thus prepared the way for the glorious epoch that was so soon to follow.

CHRISTOPH MARTIN WIELAND

FRIEDRICH GOTTLIEB KLOPSTOCK

CHAPTER VIII.

THE CLASSICAL PERIOD.

The Latter Half of the Eighteenth and the First Few Years of the Nineteenth Century

FRIEDERICH GOTTLIEB KLOPSTOCK.

High above these lesser minds arose a poet whose epic, *Der Messias,* began to appear in the *Bremer Beiträge* in 1748, without the name of the author, who proved to be FRIEDRICH GOTTLIEB KLOPSTOCK (1724-1803), the pioneer in the great classical period of German literature.

He was born in Quedlinburg, where, under the care of pious parents, he received his early education. At the age of sixteen he entered the school of Pforte, where he remained six years. While here he read Milton's *Paradise Lost,* and at once determined to write a similar epic. At **Education** the University of Jena, which he entered as a student of theology in 1745, he wrote the first three cantos of his epic in prose, because he had not yet come to a decision about the use of rhyme.

At Leipzig, whither he went in the second year of his university study, he decided on the verse of Homer, and then transferred *Messias* from prose to hexameters. When the first three cantos appeared in the *Bremer Beiträge,* they caused a sensation in Germany and in Switzerland. Bodmer saw the dream of his life fulfilled, and at once invited the young poet to his home. Although the invitation was not **At Zurich** accepted immediately, it led to Klopstock's visit later on. The old man who had so often been a friend to young poets, gave him a cordial welcome; but he was soon disappointed; for the reckless, jovial nature of his guest did not at all correspond to his own staid and sober character. He was, furthermore, grieved by the carelessness

71

with which his guest continued his great poem. The work was completed in 1773, twenty-five years after the appearance of the first cantos. He remained in Switzerland eight months, and during this time the gap between him and Bodmer became so wide that he finally took quarters in the city; yet a reconciliation was brought about before he left Zurich.

A kind invitation from the king of Denmark, accompanied by the proffer of a pension, that he might have time to complete his great work, led him to Copenhagen. On the way northward he stopped at Hamburg, met Meta Moller, whom he married in 1754, but whom he was doomed to lose four years afterward. Copenhagen was his home until 1771, when he settled in Hamburg to remain there until he died at the age of seventy-nine.

At Copenhagen

At Hamburg

Patriotism was a strong element in his character, and this love of country was what made him such a power in the development of the national literature. His great advocacy of liberty aroused his sympathies for the American Revolution, and hearty was his rejoicing at its final triumph. The beginning of the French Revolution, also, he greeted with enthusiasm and celebrated in poetry. Like Schiller, he was honored with French citizenship; but, once more like Schiller, he lost all sympathy with the revolutionists when they went to the extreme of regicide.

Political ideas

The *Messias,* in twenty long cantos, describes the plan of salvation through Christ. The poem opens in heaven, where God the Father and God the Son are in consultation; the latter declares himself ready to be sacrificed, and the former promises to forgive the sins of believers. The second canto carries the reader into hell, and shows Satan and his angels planning to kill the Messiah. Hell is described in detail, as is also heaven in the first canto. The scene of the third canto is on earth, and the disciples are introduced. Then follow the sufferings of the Saviour in Gethsemane, the betrayal by Judas, the trial before Caiaphas and Pilate, the crucifixion, the resurrection, and the ascension. It is the story of the gospels, changed and enlarged to suit the author's fancy.

Estimate of the Messias The time covered in the poem is short, beginning only a few days before the crucifixion and ending with the Lord's ascension and glorification. The subject matter of the poem is largely the invention of the poet, and deals with the transactions which he imagines to take place in the spiritual world at the same time that the events of the gospel narrative occur on earth. Although the poet has enlarged and developed the gospel story to suit his fancy, the poem is sadly lacking in action. This was due not so much to the lofty subject as to a peculiarity of the author who, as Schiller says, "lived in the realm of ideas, and who knew how to carry everything that he treated, out into the infinite." To this is doubtless due the fact that no one of the characters in the poem impresses itself upon the mind of the reader as a real creation. In place of action, feeling or emotion is prominent, which exhausts itself in exclamations at the insufficiency of human language to represent things divine, and in these exclamations the angels take part in long and wearisome speeches which delay the progress of the action in a tiresome manner. Yet notwithstanding these facts, the *Messias* is, in the words of Herder, "next to Luther's Bible, the first classic book of the German language." Furthermore it contains many beautiful passages which make it worthy of reading to-day.

In lyric poetry Klopstock's genius is at its best, and in his odes and songs the inmost reflections of his soul appear. In them he sings of friendship, love, nature, fatherland—and in it all we hear the tones of religious enthusiasm.

Lyrics These odes are for the most part written in the various meters of the ancients, a fact that forbade their ever becoming popular. Even this, however, was not without its benefits, because it attracted the minds from the dry formalism which had held sway for so long, and directed attention to the contents or thought of poetry. Only in his spiritual songs did he use rhyme, which he thought would help to make them attractive to the people in devotional service; yet only one of these ever became a popular hymn, because they were too rhetorical, and because their pure and pious thought was obscured by laborious and artificial phraseology. Patriotism, too, was the motive in many of his odes, and the same desire to glorify the greatness of **Dramas** his German fatherland led to dramatizing several historical events. Although as dramas they were absolute failures, they did have influence in awakening and strengthening the national self-consciousness.

In spite of all the criticism heaped upon him, in **Place in** spite of the fact that his works are seldom read, **literature** his poetry was the dawn of a new time, and is sufficient to immortalize his name in German letters. He was the genuine German poet, and in this respect was the forerunner of Schiller. He opened the way for the great men who followed him, and although but little read, scholars esteem him highly.

Klopstock's bold example could not fail to call **Imitators** forth imitation. Numerous indeed were the **of Klop-** men who came to the surface, only soon to dis- **stock** appear; but out of this number were a select few whose imitation opened the way for grander and for independent development. The most important and by far the most enthusiastic disciples of Klopstock are to be found in the HAINBUND (grove-league), a literary society composed of several Göttingen students who were his admirers. The real leader among them was Voss, whose description of the organization of the Bund is as follows:—

"Upon a beautiful evening we were taking a walk to a neighboring village, and were enjoying the beautiful nature around us. As we entered an oak grove, the idea came into our minds to form a league of friendship under the beautiful trees. We adorned our hats with oak leaves, laid them under one of the trees, took one another by the hand, danced around the tree, called on the moon and stars to witness the founding of the league, and promised one another an everlasting friendship." Thus arose the club whose members agreed to "spread religion, virtue, emotion, and pure innocent wit."

The nominal head of the league was CHRISTIAN BOIE, whose *Musenalmanach* practically became the organ of the league. The real head, however, was Klopstock, to whom the young "Bards of the Hain" had attached themselves from the beginning. His birthday was celebrated in a hearty manner, and his style was before them as they wrote. A great day it was, when their master visited them in 1774. Soon after this the league ceased to exist, because its members had become scattered.

The most important member of the "Hainbund" was JOHANN HEINRICH VOSS (1751-1826). He was born amid humble surroundings at Sommersdorf. While a student at the gymnasium, he gathered around him a number of his schoolmates for private study of the classics and of German literature; he also studied Klopstock, and began to imitate him. At Göttingen he devoted his attention to ancient and modern languages, and joined in the organization of the "Hainbund," although he was more independent and free from Klopstock's influence than any of the others. Having gained control of the *Musenalmanach,* he settled in Wandsbeck, married Boie's sister Ernestine, and enjoyed there several years of quiet, happy life. In 1782, he took charge of the gymnasium in Eutin, of which he was, for twenty years, the honored principal.

Being retired on a good pension, he went to Jena, and there became acquainted with Goethe and Schiller. He soon moved to Heidelberg, where he remained, in informal connection with the university, until his death.

In all his works Voss shows himself a master of language, but his imaginative faculty was weak. A didactic and often combative tone frequently appears in his odes and songs, a fact that has prevented even those works which he wrote for the people from becoming popular. Of more importance are his idyls, in which he portrays the quiet country life and the simple attractiveness of nature in northern Germany. Many a well-drawn picture has he left us, too, of the tradesman with his dressing gown and slippers. His best production, however, is *Luise,* a poem composed of three idyls.

Idyls

The first, "The Holiday in the Forest," describes in long-drawn-out details, the birthday celebration of LUISE, the daughter of the parson of Grünau. Here, in a simple and tasteful manner, he portrays the origin of Luise's love to WALTER, a student for the ministry. In the second idyl, "The Visit," Walter has become a pastor, is engaged to Luise, and is enjoying a visit at the parsonage in Grünau. The third, "The Marriage," describes the preparations for the wedding, the ceremony, the banquet, and other festivities.

The various personages of the poem do not stand out as well-defined individuals, and not one of them makes a lasting impression on the mind of the reader. Great care has been spent on the description of the locality and the outward surroundings; it is a faithful picture of the culture, the habits, and the costumes of the middle class in the eighteenth century; and furthermore, it is a good study of the ministerial calling of that time.

Translations

As a translator, Voss surpassed all his predecessors, and his best work in this line is the rendering of Homer. His version is natural and straightforward, and reproduces, to a reasonable extent, the style of the original; the Homeric formulas and epithets are successfully preserved, and the whole work is one of devoted industry and careful study.

MATTHIUS CLAUDIUS (1740-1815), although not belonging to the "Hainbund," was intimately associated with its members. After theological and law studies in Jena, he served for some time as secretary in Copenhagen, where he became acquainted with Klopstock and through him learned to appreciate Shakespeare. Returning to Hamburg, he wielded a strong influence through the publication of *Der Wansbecker Bote.*

GOTTFREID AUGUST BÜRGER (1747-94) bore somewhat the same relation to the "Hainbund." Although he wasted most of his time as a student, he finally rose to a professorship at Göttingen. His life was wild and unhappy, and before he was fifty, he died broken in body, heart, and spirit. His *Lenore,* probably the first ballad in the language, has won for him a name among literary men. Other well-known ballads are: *Kaiser und Abt* (Emperor and Abbot), *Lied vom braven Mann* (Song of the Upright Man), *Die Kuh* and *Der wilde Jäger* (The Wild Huntsman).

CHRISTOPH MARTIN WIELAND.

CHRISTOPH MARTIN WIELAND (1733-1813) was born at Oberholzheim, near Biberach. After careful and thorough training under the instruction of his father, he entered the Institute at Klosterberg near Magdeburg. While at school here Klopstock's great work appeared, and Wieland's own words tell us of the impression it made upon him: "When I read the *Messias,* I thought that I for the first time had gained a knowledge of myself." Also in Tübingen, whither he went to study law, he was influenced by Klopstock, and in imitation of him he wrote a didactic poem, *Die Natur der Dinge* (The Nature of Things). Bodmer, to whom he had sent some of his poetry, invited him to his home in Zurich. At the age of nineteen the young student accepted the invitation, and by his quiet, enthusiastic, and well-regulated life, he completely won the

Influence of Klopstock

heart of the old patron of poetry. A series of pious poems served to increase still more the admiration of his friend.

At Bern   For a short time he was a private tutor in Bern, where a marked change in his thought and life became prominent. This change passed into the extreme of frivolity when he went to Biberach, where he became a gov-

At Biberach   ernment official in 1760. Here he found a social circle whose influence made a change in his conduct and in his thinking. He now became acquainted with English and French literature, mingled in good society, and learned real life. To his new ideas he gave clever and attractive expression in a series of fantastic stories and novels which were in marked contrast to his earlier ideals. The works are filled with glaring sensuality; and were regarded as especially seductive because they were written in attractive, clever, and brilliant language.

At Weimar   After lecturing for three years at the University of Erfurt, as professor of philosophy and literature, he was called in 1772 to Weimar as the private tutor of the young prince, Karl August, who two years later took charge of the government. Thus Wieland was the first of that grand and great group of men who for so long made the little city on the Ilm the center of German literary life; made it, as it has been so often called, the "Athens of Germany." Very early in his Weimar career he began the publication of *Der deutsche Merkur* (German Mercury), a literary magazine. His aim was to make it a critical organ to which great men should contribute; but he found them not so ready to contribute as he had hoped, and he was forced to do most of the writing himself. Many of his own works first appeared in the magazine. Even after the prince attained his majority, Wieland enjoyed a pension, and remained in Weimar actively engaged in literary work until his death.

Relations to Goethe

Before Goethe came to Weimar, there existed a coolness between him and Wieland; but this turned into the warmest friendship after they were brought together in personal relations. The feeling of envy was foreign to Wieland, and the unlimited favors heaped by his pupil, Karl August, on Goethe, never aroused his jealousy. With Herder, too, he was on most intimate terms. Of these numerous literary opponents, the young bards of the "Hainbund" were the most bitter in their attacks. They had bound themselves to nourish and protect national literature, and because he admired French and English literature, they accused him of imitation, frivolity, and bad taste.

Honors

His last years were spent in quiet retirement, and yet great honors were continually bestowed upon him. In 1808 Napoleon visited him, and passed an hour in earnest conversation with him, and later sent him the Cross of the Legion of Honor. Goethe's eulogy, delivered in the Masonic Lodge, paid tribute to his colleague's kindly and friendly character. He was a perfect gentleman; and although his intellect and genius may not have been as great as those of some of his contemporaries, he was the truest of society poets, a man who did the most to please and amuse his readers.

Translations

His literary work was enormous, filling forty-two volumes. He is one of the foremost translators Germany has had. He was the first to make Shakespeare known in Germany, having translated twenty-two plays, all in prose except *Midsummer Night's Dream,* which is in the meter of the original. He did a similar work with the satires of Horace and the letters of Cicero. Among his own works several novels are prominent. Many of them are located in Greece, with classic design but modern in thought and color. Although his novels can not be called indecent, they frequently border on an undue indulgence of the amorous foibles of both sexes. Best among

these is *Die Abderiten* (1774), which will ever remain one
of the classic representations of the narrow life in a little
German town of the eighteenth century, with all its self-
importance, its insipidity, and humor. The most humorous
episode in the book is the lawsuit about a donkey's shadow,
which gradually interests and arouses the whole town, until
the factions are so angry as to lose nearly all self-control.
When the philosopher Democritus returns to Abdera after
some twenty years of travel, he is welcomed with all sorts of
questions about the marvelous sights he has seen; and when
he replies that he has beheld no giants or dwarfs, no one-
eyed or four-footed men, the people are thoroughly disgusted
with him.

His greatest work is the romantic poem OBERON (1780),
which was everywhere regarded as a masterpiece. Goethe
was so pleased that he sent a laurel wreath as a sign of
his admiration, and he wrote a friend: "As long as poetry
is poetry, gold gold, and crystal crystal, *Oberon* will be
loved and admired as a masterpiece of art." The material
is taken largely from the old French romance *Huon de Bor-
deaux;* but with this element is woven much from Shakespeare's *Midsummer Night's Dream,* and Chaucer's *Merchant's
Tale.*

The knight HÜON, who in self defense has killed, without
knowing him, the son of Charlemagne, is sent by the emperor to
Bagdad, there to accomplish a seemingly impossible deed, as a
means of reconciliation. He is to make his way into the festal
hall of the Caliph, and strike off the head of the guest at the
Caliph's left hand.

> "Then to the right draw near, with courtly grace
> The beauteous heiress of his throne embrace,
> And thrice with public kiss salute her as thy bride."

To crown the bold deed, he is to ask the Caliph for four of
his teeth, and a handful of hair from his gray beard, as a present
for the great emperor. Hüon arrives in that distant quarter of

the globe, and finds a hermit, who proves to be SHERASMIN, his father's faithful servant, who had been left behind from one of the crusades. They both set out to accomplish the undertaking, and are met in a forest by OBERON, the king of the elfs. Oberon, who had quarreled with his wife, had made a vow not to become reconciled with her until he had found a loving pair who would prefer death to separation. Since he anticipates such a pair in Hüon and the Caliph's daughter, he offers himself as a protecting spirit, and gives him a horn whose softer tones will compel all those who hear them to dance, and whose harsher tones will summon Oberon.

By the management of Oberon, Hüon on his arrival at Bagdad sees his future loved one, the charming Rezia; and she at the same time dreams of Hüon, and is filled with deep aversion toward the degenerate prince who has been thought of for her. The latter, however, is the man who sits at the left of the Caliph, as Hüon presses into the festal hall. A blow strikes his head from his body, and as the Saracens are on the point of rushing upon the stranger, their desire for revenge is turned into a desire for dancing, by the influence of the mystic horn. Oberon, who has secured the desired teeth and the handful of hair, helps the lovers out of the room, and carries them away by magic. Then he accompanies them to a ship upon which they are to return to Europe. But they do not keep the vow made to Oberon, and are married before they reach Rome, where the Pope was to bless them; for this breach of faith they are compelled to pass through trials and suffering before they attain happiness. They come from the struggle victorious; after being wrecked at sea, they reach a desert island, and Rezia says, "My heart tells me, and I believe it, that the hand which thus far has guided us will not now desert us; yet if hope grows weak, let us remember that a single moment can change everything." With a hermit they find refuge, and enjoy their quiet life and their son. But one day when he wanders from her sight, and when she is seeking him, she is carried off by pirates to the harem of King Almansor in Tunis. Hüon, who has been unable to save his wife, was bound by the pirates to a tree and left to die. Through Oberon's assistance he finally reaches Tunis, and once more sees his wife. But they have to pass through many trials, and only after they

6

have preferred death to separation, is the quarrel between Oberon
and Titania ended. The reconciled couple rescue them from
their impending danger. When the happy couple reaches home,
they are warmly welcomed by Charlemagne.

Old age
Oberon was Wieland's last great work, and
during the rest of his life he did little except
edit his works, and make some translations from Latin. His
last twenty-five years were spent in the leisurely contemplation of the development of the glorious period of German
literature, which had its center in the quartet of writers in

Place in the Weimar quartet
Weimar. He himself was the first one to come
to the little "Athens," and it was he who had
trained the young prince who afterward became
the wise and liberal patron of poetry. His works
were widely read when Herder began his critical studies.
He had watched the beginning, the rise, and the early end
of Schiller's career, and the whole broad expanse of Goethe's gigantic mind lay demonstrated before him. He was
a student when Lessing's career began, and although his life
was extended more than a quarter of a century beyond Lessing's, he belongs rather to an earlier period, and he has but
little to do with the reforms that Lessing brought about.

Service to German literature
His service to German literature, however, is
very great, and the chief points may be summed
up as follows: (1) in place of Klopstock's exag-
gerated pathos and stiffness, he imparted to the
language ease, grace, and smoothness, so that the higher
classes turned from French to their own language; (2) he
restored rhyme, which Klopstock had despised, to its proper
place; (3) he brought into favor German irony, wit, and
humor; (4) he introduced romance into German poetry.

GOTTHOLD EPHRAIM LESSING.

GOTTHOLD EPHRAIM LESSING (1729-81), the oldest of
ten sons of a pious Lutheran preacher, was born at Kamenz.
Two daughters made a complete dozen in the parson's

home. At the age of five, his joy was in books, and only
when surrounded with books was he willing to have his
portrait painted. His early education was so well cared
for by his father, and by a private tutor, and at the city
School days   school, that when he entered the royal school
at Meissen, he was far ahead of the boys of his
own age. Here he struck out in an independent course, read
a large number of Greek and Latin authors not in the
curriculum, worked at a history of mathematics among the
ancients, studied dramatic art in the dramas of Plautus
and Terence, but at the same time busied himself with the
literature of his own time. His study of Latin comedy led
him to attempt something of the same kind, and *Der junge
Gelehrte* (Young Scholar) was the result.

University life   At the age of seventeen he entered the university at Leipzig to follow his father's wish in
studying theology. But he felt more inclined
toward philosophy, literature, and mathematics, and the
lively city itself inspired him, since, as he wrote to his
mother, "there one could see the whole world on a small
scale." Along with his studies he took an interest in ath-
letics. The theater had a strong hold upon him. He ate
dry bread rather than miss the play; often he would translate French pieces for tickets to the theater. This influence
led him to rearrange *Der junge Gelehrte* for the stage, and
he had the pleasure of seeing it played and well received.
This was the first of a whole series of comedies that came
from his pen. All this in addition to his companionship
with MYLIUS, a cultured free thinker, led his parents to call
him home for a short time. But when they saw that his
character was still pure and untainted, and that he had
done good work, they consented to his giving up theology
and entering medicine. Returning to Leipzig, he took up
his scientific studies with great industry, but still was a
constant attendant at the theater. Unfortunately his inti-

macy with the actors led him to go security for some of them, who left him to pay their bills. Hard pressed by his creditors, he went to Wittenberg to continue his studies, but sickness overtook him. His creditors were soon pressing him hard again, and he decided to give up his studies.

He went to Berlin and, through the influence of his friend Mylius, obtained a position with a newspaper, for which he wrote editorials, articles on scientific subjects, and prepared translations from foreign languages. Before long he became tired of this trying work, and then returned to Wittenberg, where he remained a year at the University and gained the degree of Master of Arts. Going back to Berlin, he resumed his former activity on the newspaper, studied English and Italian, prepared translations from these languages, and was active in both scientific and poetical work.

At the beginning of 1755, he retired to a secluded house in Potsdam, where he remained several weeks developing material for a drama which he had had in mind for a long time. The result was *Miss Sara Sampson,* the success of which aroused all the poet's longing for connection with a theater, and since Frederick the Great's preference for French had stifled every effort at German dramatic art in Berlin, Lessing went once more to Leipzig, where he lived in the theater as he had done in his student days. *Sara Sampson* was rearranged and successfully presented, and the author in all the glow of early success, began a series of dramas; but before any of them were finished, he started on a journey over half of Europe, as traveling companion to a rich young man. They had just finished Holland when Frederick the Great's invasion of Saxony called him home.

Hard times stared him in the face, and he found himself compelled to earn his bread by literary work, by translations, and by teaching. After a year's activity in various kinds of literary work in Berlin, he suddenly and without the knowledge of his friends accepted a call to Breslau as

At Breslau government secretary. Here he spent five years, which, in spite of his unattractive duties and all kinds of social distractions, were very important for his development. Furthermore, since he did not have to write for his bread, he wrote much more freely and with more vigor. During this time, he began *Minna von Barnhelm* and *Laokoon*.

Growing tired of his irksome tasks, he returned to Berlin, and for a while occupied himself with finishing the *Litteraturbriefe*.

A reward for his work now seemed to be in store for him. A librarian was to be chosen for the royal library in Berlin, and Lessing was highly recommended. Frederick the Great, however, preferred a Frenchman. The great scholar was painfully disappointed in this. There was no longer any attraction for him in the capital, and he accepted

At Hamburg a call to take charge of a German national theater in Hamburg, whither he went in 1767, and where *Minna von Barnhelm* was first presented. All his energy was devoted to his new work, but once more the unfortunate man was doomed to disappointment, as the management failed financially, and was unable to pay him his salary or the royalty for his plays. From a literary standpoint this year was quite important, for it produced the *Hamburgische Dramaturgie*.

While in Hamburg, Lessing moved among the best society, and was always a welcome guest at the homes of the foremost families of the city. Especially was he intimate at the home of Engelbert KÖNIG, whose gifted widow, Eva, several years later, became Lessing's wife. When her husband died at Venice, Lessing was the truest of friends to the widow and her orphan children; but not until much later, after he had gone from Hamburg to Wolfenbüttel, did love spring up between them. In 1770 he was

**At Wolfen-
büttel** called to Wolfenbüttel as librarian. A miserable position it was, with a salary of $450 in an out-of-the-way little town. Yet he had time for writing, and his betrothal with Eva served to gladden his seclusion. *Emilia Galotti* was completed in 1772. Now an opportunity came for him to satisfy his desire for travel. He accompanied the Prince of Brunswick on a trip through Vienna to Italy. Although they visited most of the cities of Italy and southern Germany, the journey was made in such haste that he had very little time to make use of it for literary development.

Promotion In the following year he received the title of "Prince's Counselor," his salary was raised, and a dwelling was given him, so that he could marry Eva. The year 1777 was the most peaceful and happy of his life, yet this domestic joy was to be of only short duration. A son, in whom were centered the poet's hopes, died the day after its birth, and, to Lessing's indescribable grief, from which he never recovered, his wife soon followed her child. Writing to one of his friends, he says, "I now wished to be as happy as other men, but sorrow is my lot." From this time on, his life was broken. Visits to Brunswick or Hamburg would recuperate and refresh him only for a time; he grew sick, and could seldom rise above the saddened tone that had come into his life. This sadness was increased by the long-continued and aggravating literary and theological disputes with several men, particularly with Pastor GOEZE, of Hamburg. This exhausting labor completely ruined his already weakened health, his eyesight began to fail him, and blindness seemed in store for him; but after a short spell of acute illness, he was relieved from his sufferings by a stroke of apoplexy, at the age of fifty-two. While in the midst of these theological disputes, he produced *Nathan der Weise*.

Intellectual character Lessing acquired an extraordinary and many-sided erudition, and possessed an insatiable desire for research. Not so much knowledge itself as the search for knowledge made him happy; to him the seeking for truth was more than the possession of truth. This characteristic explains his study on all branches of science, esthetics, philology, literature, archæology, theology, and also his comparatively short devotion to each. To this is due the fragmentary nature of much that he wrote, as well as the restlessness that characterized him through his life; and the same trait explains his dislike for authority which checked him in his original research. But in whatever realm he worked, there his extraordinary power and keenness of mind were ever most productive.

A critic Macaulay calls him the "greatest critic of Europe," and in these words he has characterized the kernel of his being and the keynote of his importance in literature. His sharp eye was on all the productions of German literature, and he says himself, "I like no more agreeable occupation than to examine the names of renowned men, to investigate their right to immortality, to remove undeserved spots and blemishes that do not belong to them." With this method he did great service in freeing German literature from the slavish admiration of foreign lands, and, furthermore, he was the first to destroy the false models on which his people hung. When he criticised, it was with rigid precision and unrelenting severity. His maxim was, "A poor poet one does not criticise at all, a mediocre, gently, but a great poet, relentlessly." Yet, while he directed his eye to the errors of others, he by no means spared himself in his criticisms, and he was free from all self-conceit.

His works Lessing towers up in German literature as a critic and as a dramatic poet. To him, next to Luther, are the Germans indebted for modern prose, and

Prose his style stands even to-day as a peerless model. From every sentence there appears the cultured training of his thoughtful mind, the craving for knowledge, the tireless energy of exact research. The sense of truth with which Lessing was endowed, the bold courage with which he entered a contest, and the sharp severity which he put into his words,—all these make his works a fresh, gushing stream. His best prose is to be found in his critical writings, of which the three most important are: *Die Litteraturbriefe, Laokoon,* and *Hamburgische Dramaturgie.*

LITTERATURBRIEFE (Literary Letters) (1759-65). According to his preface, these letters were written as if addressed to a cultured Prussian officer who had been wounded, and who was recuperating in a little town. The letters were supposed to have been written by friends with a view to filling up the gaps in his knowledge of the newest literature. With inconsiderate boldness, he discusses the principal productions of contemporary literature, the whole of which he always had under his eye. It was his care to free literature of all that was not pure, and of all that was not German. The bad taste of the poor translators and of the professional scribblers, he took delight in exposing. The seventeenth letter is directed against Gottsched, whose use of French formality and translation of French dramas he regarded as a backward step in the development of the German drama, which should be modeled on the masterpieces of Shakespeare as we see from the following:—

"To decide the matter even according to the ancients, Shakespeare is a much greater tragic poet than Corneille, although the latter was well acquainted with the classics, while the former was not. Corneille approaches them more nearly in the mechanical arrangement, while Shakespeare comes nearer to them in the essentials of poetry. The Englishman reaches the goal of tragedy most always, in however peculiar and characteristic ways he may choose, and the Frenchman seldom reaches it, although he follows the well-defined rules of the ancients. After the *Oedipus* of Sophocles, no other drama in the world can have more influence over our passions than *Othello, King Lear,* or *Hamlet.*"

LAOKOON; or, *On the Limits of Painting and Poetry* (1766). In 1506 in the house of the Emperor Titus at Rome, there was discovered a Greek marble statue, which is among the most beautiful of ancient works of art. It represents the Trojan priest Laokoon, as he and his two sons are being killed by two snakes at the command of Poseidon, because he had warned his countrymen of the wooden horse of the Greeks. In an article on *The Imitation of Greek Works in Painting and Sculpture,* WINCKELMANN[1] had compared this marble group with Virgil's description in the second book of the Æneid, and had maintained that in the statue the priest gave vent to no horrible cry, as Virgil attributes to him, but only sighed and thereby showed himself a hero who could endure excruciating pain without groaning. This comparison led Lessing to express his opposing opinions and to prove that the realm of painting (under this term he included sculpture) and of poetry, were widely separated from each other. He maintains, next, that the suppression of a cry of pain does not testify of an especially strong soul —the heroes of all Greek poets would have cried. Therefore some other reason must have led the sculptor to differ from the poet. This lies in the difference between the formative and the descriptive arts. Both are subject to the law of beauty, but each must satisfy that law in its own way. The painter and the sculptor, whose realm is space,

---

[1]Winckelmann was born in 1717 at Stendel as the son of a poor shoemaker. After studying at Halle and Jena, he obtained a position near Dresden which gave him opportunity to study art. Soon he was filled with a desire to go to Italy, the classic home of plastic art. His conversion to Catholicism aided him in his purpose. In Florence, Naples, and Rome, he continued the studies which gave rise to his *History of Ancient Art* (1764), in which he first opened the way for comprehending the art of antiquity. After a long residence in Rome he returned to Germany, but remained only a short time.

can choose only one moment for representation, and must choose this moment so that it will occupy the imagination of the beholder, and yet not offend his feeling of beauty. On the other hand, succession in time is the field of the poet; therefore he can allow a series of moments to be brought to our notice, and may properly weave into his poetry the violent, the disagreeable, the cry of pain, because it is so softened and so reconciled by what follows, that it does not offend the reader's feeling of beauty. For this reason, then, the sculptor had to soften Laokoon's cries to sighs; not because a cry betrays an ignoble soul, but because it would distort the face in an offensive manner. Painting and sculpture represent bodies by their attributes, poetry by actions. And when poetry wishes to represent bodies, it can do it only by allusion through continuous action.

The first part of the sixteenth chapter is devoted to a summary of the principles discussed, and the latter part shows how they harmonize with the practice of Homer, who represents everything by progressive action. If he describes at all, it is by a single epithet,—choosing that which is most suggestive,—or by giving, instead of a description of the object itself, the narrative of its growth; he follows it through the various stages of its history or development, and by these means,—by presenting action to the mind of the reader—he succeeds in producing a very lively idea in his mind. The chariot of Juno is put together piece by piece; we see the wheels made, the tongue attached, and all the details of the operation. We see Agamemnon putting on his garments one after the other; and we follow his scepter from the tree on which it grew, through all the royal hands that wielded it, and we are more impressed with its importance than by a minute description of the thing itself.

DIE HAMBURGISCHE DRAMATURGIE (Hamburg Dramaturgy) was a semi-weekly journal devoted to the interests of the Hamburg National Theater and written by Lessing himself. The actors, wishing to be praised, disliked his criticsms, and the public, not being interested in the subject, soon failed to give it financial support. After a struggle of two years the *Dramaturgie,* which had ceased criticising the performances regularly, and had introduced the general discussion of dramatic questions instead, was given up. But these two volumes are of great value; they are rich in information about the plays of the time, rich in discerning criticism of dramatic art and dramatic poetry in general. These volumes became the foundation for the reform of the German theater, and in them were arranged, in a **Dramatic** more careful and concise form than ever before, **laws** the laws of the drama. The German stage was at that time overrun with French pieces; of the seventy-five dramas upon which Lessing reports, fifty-two were from the French. The French had been, up to this time, regarded as excellent models, because it was supposed that their dramas were written in accordance with the rules of the Greeks, as they had been arranged by Aristotle; Corneille, Racine, and Voltaire were regarded as the disciples and followers of Æschylus and Sophocles, and to imitate the French was regarded as working according to the rules of the ancients. He opposes the strict adherence by the French to the three unities of the classic drama: action, place, and time. Of these he maintains that only the first is essential, while the other two are to be respected only so far as is demanded by the first. Here, even more emphatically than in the *Litteraturbriefe,* did he recommend Shakespeare as the source from which the Germans should draw their inspiration in dramatic literature.

A dramatic poet Lessing is by no means of less importance as a dramatist. Although he himself thought very little of his qualifications in this line, he has left the following works of lasting influence and imperishable worth: *Miss Sara Sampson, Minna von Barnhelm, Emilia Galotti,* and *Nathan der Weise.*

By choosing for Miss Sara Sampson an English subject

and writing it in prose, Lessing broke away from French traditions, but he produced a drama lively in action and true to life.

SARA SAMPSON is enticed from home by the profligate MELL-FORT through promise of marriage. Although he really loves her, he hesitates to marry her because he dreads the restraints of married life, and because he is in some sense bound to a former loved one, MRS. MARWOOD. Yet he can not part from Sara even when MRS. MARWOOD follows him, and tries to win him back, avenging herself by poisoning her rival. Sara's father overtakes and forgives his dying daughter, and the murderess escapes.

MINNA VON BARNHELM (1767) is in entire harmony with the requirements of the *Litteraturbriefe*, and was really the first national drama, dealing with contemporary events. The scene is laid in Berlin, after the Seven Years' War; the characters no longer bear Greek or Latin names, and are not mere masks, but are living people with well-defined traits. From beginning to end it is full of German life, German love, and German action. The fact that it was built upon the national background of the war which was still fresh in the minds of all, had much to do with its influence upon high and low. It is popular in the best sense of the word. Especially gratifying is the reconciliation between the two German races, who had for so long been hostile to each other, and who in the Prussian Major von Tellheim and in Saxon Minna von Barnhelm extend, as it were, to each other, the hand in peace.

During the Seven Years' War, MAJOR VON TELLHEIM, a Prussian officer, is sent into Saxony to raise war contributions. Finding it impossible to extort the required amounts from the impoverished people, he furnishes the deficiency from his own resources. This gains him the admiration and love of a wealthy Saxon heiress, MINNA VON BARNHELM and they become engaged. After the declaration of peace Tellheim with many other officers is retired on half pay, and to add to his embarrassment, he is unjustly suspected of having allowed himself to be bribed by the Saxons. Thus deeply mortified and financially embarrassed, he thinks he must renounce Minna, and without giving her any information of himself, he goes to Berlin, where he lives in seclusion in a modest hotel with his rough yet honorable and good-hearted servant JUST. His former servant, PAUL WERNER, sells his estate, and brings the proceeds to Tellheim for him to keep and use, but the Major refuses to take it.

As his embarrassment increases, he pawns the engagement ring which Minna had given him. Shortly before this, she had come to Berlin to hunt her lover, and accidentally put up at the same hotel. Out of curiosity, the landlord shows her the ring, through which she at once comprehends Tellheim's presence and his straitened circumstances. She redeems the treasure, and, with the help of her sly and merry companion, FRANZISKA, she sets herself about trying to change her lover's purpose, by pretending that she has been disinherited. As strongly as he had refused to marry the rich Minna, so strongly he now determines to marry the disinherited Minna. Now just as the conflict between honor and love is settled, the decision of the court is announced, and a letter from the king re-establishes Tellheim's honor. Minna's uncle comes in time to welcome the Major as his son, and the difficulty is very happily solved. Werner, too, is happy, having found in Franziska a neat little woman, whom he marries. By way of contrast to the honest German character, there is introduced a contemptible Frenchman, who amuses the audience with his broken German.

Estimate With one exception the characters are excellent, lovable, and thoroughly German. The drama is an homage to German women, a glorification of the Prussian army, and a eulogy of the king, who looms up in the background as the administrator of that justice which restores to the Major his lost pride, vindicates his honor, and brings everything to a happy end. The whole is embodied in scenes, partly mirthful, partly affecting. This first German comedy, with its German characters, written in fresh dialogue and striking humor, soon became popular on all the stages of Germany, and is popular to-day.

EMILIA GALOTTI (1772). As early as 1758 Lessing had planned a tragedy on the basis of the well-known Roman story of "Virginia," and at first he expected to make it extol an uprising in the cause of liberty; but later he stripped it of its ancient coloring, and made it represent the court of one of the contemporary Italian princes.

EMILIA, the daughter of ODOARDO GALOTTI and the betrothed of COUNT APPIANI, on her wedding day, rushes into the house with the news that PRINCE VON GUASTALLA had declared his love for her. Following the advice of her mother, she says nothing to her father or lover about the matter. Although the prince knows that nothing short of a crime can let him carry out his purpose, he allows his chamberlain, the coming MARINELLI, to plan for setting Appiani aside. After he refuses to accept an appointment as ambassador to a foreign court, murder seems the only way to get rid of him. The carriage which is conveying the bridal pair to the church is attacked by hired bandits, Appiani is shot, and Emilia is carried to the prince's palace by servants, who pretend that they are rescuers. With all appearances of horror and surprise, the prince receives her, assures her of his sympathy, and promises to search out the murderers. When her parents come for her, hindrances are put in the way, and they are told that, for the sake of a careful search for the murderers, they must be separated from their daughter. In the meantime one of the prince's jilted sweethearts, COUNTESS ORSINA, tells the father the true state of affairs. Odoardo is finally given permission to speak to his daughter, and he then tells her how the matter stands. They see no other way of rescuing her from shame than by her death. She perceivs that the prince has had some influence over her, she longs for death, and at her request, her father plunges a dagger into her heart.

The characters are well drawn; the worthy old father, rough and impetuous; the honest, manly lover; the charming, modest girl, who in her timidity is the most resolute of

her sex; the profligate prince, whose mind is open to the
higher interests of refinement, but who never restrains his
wishes, because he thinks himself subject to no law; even
the less prominent characters are graphically presented,
and the course of the action springs, according to the principles of the *Dramaturgie,* from the nature of the characters. The plot is developed without awkward halts or gaps.
As *Minna* proved Lessing to be a master of comedy, so this
piece proved him to be a master of tragedy, and both show
him to be the teacher of dramatic writing in the Germany
of his day. In spite of the Italian dress, the play is German throughout, for there were at that time numerous Guas-
tallas and Marinellis in Germany.

NATHAN DER WEISE (Nathan the Wise, 1779) is a hymn
of all-embracing human love, and it is written in the grace
and charm of rhythm, while his former works are in prose.
It is a didactic piece, through which Lessing wished to preach
toleration in religious beliefs.

The scene is laid in Jerusalem, where, at the time of the
Crusades, Christian, Jew, and Mussulman were to be found together. There it happened that ASSAD, brother of the Sultan
SALADIN, on account of his love for a Christian girl of noble
rank, was converted to Christianity. His son was sent to Germany to be educated, and there he became a Templar. Immediately after the birth of their second child, the mother died,
leaving a baby girl whom her father sent to his friend, the rich
merchant Nathan, to be cared for during his absence in the war.
He, however, was killed, and Nathan, with the help of the child's
Christian nurse, brought her up as his own daughter in his own
faith, giving her the name of RECHA. Just as she was entering
on young womanhood, she was rescued from the flames by a
Templar. The Templar who had been condemned to death,
is pardoned by the sultan, his features reminding him of the
brother whom he had lost years before. Nathan, returning from
a business trip, wins the Templar's confidence and welcomes
him to his house, where he becomes acquainted with Recha, and

loves her. When Nathan hesitates about giving him Recha as
his wife, the Templar is much provoked, and since he has
learned from the nurse that Recha is not the daughter of Nathan, but is descended from Christian parents, he determines to
lay the matter before the Patriarch. After he has presented
an imaginary case to him, and has learned that burning would
be in store for Nathan if his name were given, he pretends that
he had no one person in mind, and changes his plans. Yet he
does not give up his hopes for Recha, and finally is helped by
the sultan and his sister. Just here, however, a priest who had
brought Recha from her father to Nathan, produces a Breviary
in Assad's own handwriting, proving that the Templar is Assad's
son and Recha's brother. Saladin at once announces them both
as his brother's children.

In this piece different nationalities and creeds are united
in peaceful and harmonious bonds, a dream that Lessing
had long cherished. Cheerful characters and incidents alter-
nate with serious and affecting ones, and this mingling of
light and shade brings the play down to the level of real life,
instead of keeping it in the realm of purely ideal deeds and
noble sentiments. One great purpose of Lessing was to
demonstrate the right of the various religions to exist. In
doing this he chose to represent each one of the three prominent religions by a concrete example, but the Jew Nathan,
the Mohammedan Saladin, and the baptized Templar are
not genuine examples of their religions. They are rather
representatives of Theism, which is founded on a general
faith in God and his control of the universe, though not by
supernatural means. They are united in looking beyond the
differences of nationalities and creeds to the common basis
of humanity, and they consider good action to be the aim in
life.

Inasmuch as Lessing has put the three religions side by
side, we may say that he has been somewhat unfair to
Christianity. The representatives of the other two religions
are thoroughly ideal characters. Nathan is a lover of hu-

GOTTHOLD EPHRAIM LESSING

JOHANN GOTTFRIED HERDER

manity. Saladin is a noble and ideal nature. With these not one of the characters that represent Christianity can be compared, not one of them portrays the Christian spirit in its purity. The Patriarch is just the opposite of our ideal of a Christian man; he is the fanatic and pious bigot who would like to drive everybody by fire and sword into conformity with his own views. The Templar is a true, noble, and heroic character, but gloomy, and religiously indifferent. Strict justice demands a Christian character worthy to stand by the side of Nathan and Saladin. Although the scene is in Jerusalem and the time that of the Crusades, the ideas of humanity and toleration by which the chief characters are controlled belong wholly to the time of the poet, and express his generosity and liberality.

Place in literature
The loss of this great reformer was felt most keenly by the great men of literature. Goethe, at the age of thirty-two, on hearing of his death, said: "We lose much in him, more than we realize." That this opinion only increased with age we may see from his remark at the age of seventy-six: "We need a man like Lessing, for he was great by his character and will-power. There are plenty of men of culture and cleverness, but where is there such a character?" As time goes on, his work becomes grander and grander, for we see him as he really was, noble, unselfish, and truth-loving; gentle and charitable to all, stern only in his hatred of cowardice, hypocrisy, and falsehood. Through his influence several reforms were brought about in German literature: the nature and laws of dramatic poetry were established; servile imitation was banished; national dramas were introduced and made popular; the way for national literary development was pointed out; religious toleration was encouraged; and the style and content of German prose was greatly improved.

7

JOHANN GOTTFRIED HERDER.

Boyhood
JOHANN GOTTFRIED HERDER (1744-1803) was the son of a school-teacher in Mohrungen in eastern Prussia, where one of his teachers became attached to him, and gave him private instruction in Greek and Hebrew. Soon he showed his desire for study, and the parson took him into his home. This gave him a chance to use a good library, and the boy made such use of it that he injured his eyesight, a fact that led him to consult a Russian surgeon who was attached to the troops quartered there. The aspiring and gifted boy interested him so much that he offered to take him to Königsberg to study medicine.

University days
Herder accepted the proposition, and began his work in preparing for the profession, but, at the first sight of a surgical operation, he fainted, and at once gave up the calling forever. He now turned his attention to theology, for which he had always had a liking. To this subject he added philosophy and philology. One of his favorite instructors was the philosopher KANT,[1] who admitted him to all his lectures free of tuition. Another man, however, whose name is scarcely known except to specialists in literature, was one of the powerful factors in making Herder what he was. This was HAMANN. Through these two men, he became acquainted with ROUSSEAU and SHAKESPEARE, and received the inspiration to the literary activity which he afterward developed. On leaving the university, he was called to Riga, where he spent five years as an efficient teacher and preacher.

Travels
Becoming tired of his work, and longing to see the world, he went by sea to Nantes, thence to

---

[1]Kant is the creator of a new system of philosophy, the father of the so-called critical philosophy. His important works are *Critique of Pure Reason* (1781), *Critique of Practical Reason* (1787), and *Critique of Judgment* (1790). He tried to prove that supersensuous things can not be known through pure reason. The ideas of God, freedom, and immortality are postulates of the practical reason (the conscience). His philosophy soon entered into all science and literature, into poetry and life. Herder, Hamann, Goethe, and Schiller especially became his admirers.

Paris, where he received the commission to accompany the Prince of Holstein-Eutin through France and Italy. He accepted the offer, and, on the way to meet the prince, he stopped at Hamburg, and spent two weeks with Lessing. While at Darmstadt, he became acquainted with CAROLINE FLACHSLAND, who later became his wife, and who was not only his home companion, but also his intellectual counselor, in full sympathy with him in all his work. At Strassburg he parted from the prince, and submitted to a surgical operation on his eyes. Here he became acquainted

Acquaint-ance with Goethe with GOETHE, who was five years his junior, and who was his constant companion during the painful confinement after the operation. Their friendship was intimate, and Goethe derived great benefit from it, as his friend had studied extensively, and was far in advance of him. In 1771 he was called to Bückeburg as court preacher, where he remained five years. In the mean-

At Weimar time, Goethe had become the intimate friend and guest of the young duke of Weimar, and was influential in securing a call for his friend Herder, as court preacher and superintendent of the church district of Weimar. In addition to his numerous and extensive official duties, he was always busy with some literary work; but notwithstanding the success of his writings, and in spite of the favor bestowed upon him by the duke, he never was perfectly satisfied. He was sensitive by nature, and often suffered from embarrassing situations, now a rupture with the Weimar society, and now a quarrel with Goethe or Schiller. A bright spot in all his troubles was the long-desired journey to Italy. After his return, he rose to the honorable position of President of the Consistory, and was ennobled by the Elector of Bavaria. Death came after a long sickness, and he was buried in the city church.

His work In his critical writings, Herder was the disciple of Lessing, enlarging and continuing his work, yet in his own peculiar way and often differing in judgment. While in Lessing keenness in intellect is ever prominent, in Herder feeling and emotion are more striking; while Lessing's language is logically precise, **Comparison** clear, and exact, Herder's is fanciful, lofty, and **with Less-** figurative. He was a careful, enthusiastic, yet **ing** critical reader of Lessing. But there was a characteristic difference; while Lessing was first and foremost an art critic, and only secondarily a historian of literature, Herder was pre-eminently a historian of literature, and only incidentally an art critic. Lessing used his knowledge of literature simply as so much material from which to find rules of composition and basis of criticism, but Herder made the study of literature an end in itself worthy of enthusiastic devotion. He strove to transfer himself to the circumstances in which literary works were produced, and to study the production from that standpoint.

In *Die kritischen Wälder* (Critical Forests), which may be regarded as a continuation of *Laokoon,* he refers to Homer as the poet of nature, in contrast to the artificial element in Virgil. In *Die Blätter von deutscher Art und Kunst* (Leaves of German Art), he points to Shakespeare as an example of the perfection that can be attained in the drama, by choosing the material from the life of the people. He shows that one important element in the work of the English poet was his creating and representing men of the North. Since he, in time, in nationality, and in intellect stands so much nearer to the Germans than the writers of antiquity, he must serve as the master in the drama.

Stimmen der Völker in Liedern (Voices of the Nations in Song) is the high-sounding title given by the publishers to a series of folksongs (1778-79) in which Herder emphatically and effectively awoke appreciation for the songs of earlier times. The collection comprises popular songs by unknown authors and characteristic songs from the literature of all nations. Every kind of lyric poetry is represented, and the only kind of classification among them is that of community of thought and sentiment. But they are not mere translations, they have sunk so deeply in the author's mind as to come forth new productions; yet even in this he has shown his appreciation of the songs by striking the right note in his reproductions, by reproducing not only the feelings, but even the peculiar meter and style of each poem. The whole collection is a series of exquisite gems of poetry.

The ripest fruit of his study of popular poetry is Herder's version of the Spanish romances which had gathered around the name of CID. According to recent researches, Herder's poem is a more or less literal, metrical rendering of a French prose treatment of the Spanish romances which date from the thirteenth, fourteenth, and fifteenth centuries. Herder has been criticised for modernizing the old hero, and thus depriving him of some of his strength; but whether this be so or not, certain it is that he has made a genuine German poem of great value, in which there is much that is original, alongside of that portion which was brought from foreign sources. The poem treats of the deeds of Rodrigo Diaz, who was called by his contemporaries "Cid el batal" (lord of battle).

I. RODRIGO's father is vexed and tormented by his enemy, DON GORMAZ, whom Rodrigo challenges to a duel, and kills. XIMENE, Gormaz's daughter, goes to the king, and begs for satisfaction; but before he can answer her request the young hero has freed his country from the destructive Moors. For this work he is given the name of CID, and in the fierce struggle he becomes indispensable. The king not only refuses to grant Ximene's request, but adds that just as ardently as she now pleads for his death, just so ardently will she soon beg for his life and welfare. The Cid has long loved Ximene, and she, after struggling hard against it, finally yields, and returns his love.

II. After the king's death, the kingdom is divided, and the Cid becomes the vassal of the eldest son, DON SANCHO, who soon attacks his brothers and sisters. Through the bravery of the Cid, his brothers are overcome, and their territory as well as that of one of the sisters, comes into the land of Sancho. But when the Cid comes to the castle of the younger sister, she reminds him that he had promised her father to protect her, at which he withdraws. Sancho is much vexed at this and banishes him from the kingdom; but soon is compelled to recall him, as after his departure, victory had deserted the royal troops. In spite of the Cid's warning, the king wishes to take his sister's city, and in the attempt he is slain by the hands of a traitor.

III. After DON ALFONSO, a younger brother, has sworn that he has had no part in the murder of Sancho, the Cid agrees to enter his service. But the new regent can not long endure the haughty demeanor of his great vassal, the CID is banished from the court, and is even robbed of all his property. Then the hero departs with his soldiers, and seeks, far away from the court of the king, to win new glory and renown.

IV. He wins brilliant victories over the Moors, levies taxes upon them, makes them render him service, and establishes his residence in Valentia. His wife and two daughters come to the new home. Old age comes upon the hero, and thirty days before his death, the apostle Peter appears to him, and announces that in a month God will summon him to the other world. He arranges his affairs, and commands his people to keep the news of his death from the Moors, who were again devastating the country. His body is embalmed, clad in all his armor, set upon his old war-horse, and thus led out of Valentia. When the Moors see him they are panic-stricken, and at once flee. Thus the Cid conquered even after death, and the king ordered that, instead of being buried, he should have a chair near the altar.

Besides the various lines of work in literature, Herder was a strong writer in numerous other subjects; to theology and philosophy, to philology and history, his contributions were of importance. In these lines his best work is *Ideen zur Philosophie der Geschichte der Menschheit* (Ideas about the Philosophy of the History of Humanity). This work represents the whole history of mankind as a series of na-

tional organisms; each independent, each following its own
spirit; each developing characteristic language, religion, society, literature, and art; and yet each by its own development enriching the human race as a whole. Every person
is an heir of all the ages, an epitome of a whole nation. It
considers man in the fullness of all his powers, and at the
same time in his endless variety of relations to those about
him. It presents history as an unbroken whole, as a chain
of cause and effect, or as a living organism in which nothing
is lost, and in which all forces are utilized. It remains un-
finished, and no longer corresponds to the present ideas of
science, but is a monument of a beginning of a more pro-
found comprehension of history. Its influence has been
enormous, and few have been the books that have wrought
on the world's culture as this. It laid the foundation upon
which scores of great thinkers have builded, so that, when
one now reads it, he finds himself already acquainted with
the ideas, inasmuch as they have been made known to the
world, not only in Germany but in other lands, by the hun-
dredfold borrowings that have been made from it. Another
work of considerable importance is *Briefe zur Beförderung
der Humanität*, containing portraits of great historical characters, whom Herder holds up as models of virtue. Chief
among these is a picture of Frederick the Great. In addition to his literary greatness, he was one of the first orators
of his time; he was enthusiastic, and could carry his enthusiasm to others.

Contribution to literature
In a remarkable degree did Herder possess the
power to comprehend the thought and the circumstances of foreign writers, and to reproduce
them with all their essential qualities; but original creative
poetic power was lacking in him. His poetry is noble in
expression, rich in earnest and deep thought, but before
everything else it is didactic. Although he was not a great
creative genius, he could feel what was beautiful, make it

his own, and reproduce it. By using this quality in his nature he has done great service in the development of German literature, and among other things should be mentioned the following facts: he established a close relation between poetry and intellect; he aroused an enthusiasm for the beautiful, by reproducing the popular poetry of many nations; he gave the Germans excellent models; he was strong in his opposition to the French influence; and as a liberal and tolerant man, he strove for liberty, truth, and justice; last, but by no means least, his services as tutor to Goethe were productive of great good.

JOHANN WOLFGANG VON GOETHE

THE GOETHE HOME AT WEIMAR

THE SCHILLER HOME AT WEIMAR

CHAPTER IX

THE CLASSICAL PERIOD—Continued

GOETHE AND SCHILLER.

Klopstock and Wieland, Lessing and Herder, opened up new fields of thought in the intellectual life of Germany. They inaugurated a movement which in the youth of the country led to a tumult, in which the young writers ran from one extreme to the other. The commotion passed throughout the cultured world; in all lands there was a revolt against the established principles of society and state, a longing to return to the natural state of mankind. The leader of the movement was without doubt the Genevese philosopher, JEAN JACQUES ROUSSEAU, in whose writings the revolutionary principles are most abundant, most radical, and the most effective. His ideas spread over Germany, where they became known through romances of adventure, and where even Klopstock led in looking back to the early life of the Germans for literary material. The real root of the agitation was Rousseau's gospel of nature. That which lay quiet and awe-inspiring in the hearts of the German youths, soon gained, through Rousseau's influence, life and consciousness, purpose and direction, form and content. The height of the period was attained during the seventies and eighties of the last century. "Originality and genius" was their watchword. In many of the writers these principles degenerated into pure license. In ridding themselves of the old laws that shackled art, they forgot those that regulated morals; they led wild and often dissipated lives, and many a gifted man lost all his poetic power in the general ruin which such ideas and habits necessarily bring with them.

One of the leaders of this fantastic literature was MAXIMILIAN KLINGER (1752-1831). He was a friend of Goethe's,

Storm and Stress

and wrote several dramas, in which he piles up horrors and regards them as everyday things. A few of them show observation and knowledge of society. The most characteristic and the best known among them is *Sturm und Drang,* the title of which soon became applied to the whole period. The plot of this one treats of the quarrel and reconciliation of two Scottish noblemen who go to America to take part in the Revolution. In later years, however, Klinger recovered from his youthful and erroneous ideas, and attained to a respectable position in the Russian army.

While so many men of genius were going to ruin through the "Storm and Stress" influence, there arose a POET-PAIR who stand out alone in German literature and in world literature, in their clearness and in their influence. GOETHE and SCHILLER, in their earlier years, both belonged to the party of genius and originality, but both overcame their youthful fancies, developed into strong, manly characters, and formed the center of the greatest period that Germany has yet known. At first they had little to do with each other, but later their lives and their work became so closely connected that we must ever think of them together, and consequently treat of their writings together.

JOHANN WOLFGANG VON GOETHE (1749-1832)
His Youth and Early Writings (1749-1775)

The times in which he lived We have now come to the greatest name in German literature, and before we look at the man and his work, let us cast a glance at the time in which his life falls, and at his endowments. His intellect was broad, ruling, and calm from its very vastness and strength. He was royally endowed by nature, and everything that cultured surroundings and easy circumstances could give him, enabled him to make free and unbounded use of his power. His long life of literary activity began just when Klopstock's influence was spreading over

Germany, and ended when the cold scientific spirit of modern times succeeded the commotion of the Storm and Stress period. His lifetime embraces many important events in the history of the world, as his own words tell us: "I had the advantage of being born when the world was agitated by great movements, which have continued during my long life; so that I am a living witness of the Seven Years' War, the American Revolution, the French Revolution, the whole Napoleonic era, with the downfall of that hero, and the events which followed. Thus I have attained results and insight impossible to those who must learn these things from books."

Boyhood GOETHE was born on the 28th of August, 1749 at Frankfort-on-the-Main. His father was a man of good education, holding the position of imperial counselor, and was in the enjoyment of a good fortune. His

His mother mother was the daughter of the town magistrate, twenty-one years younger than her husband, and the ideal woman for a poet's mother. She is one of the most attractive women connected with German literature, and stands out more distinctly than almost any other. She was simple, hearty, joyous, and affectionate, the delight of children, the favorite of poets and princes. She was only eighteen when the poet was born, and instead of making her old, this seems to have kept her young. "I and my Wolfgang," she says, "have always held together, because we were young together." From her he inherited the love of story-telling, physical vivacity, distinctive individuality, and especially the love of seeing happy faces around him. His sister, CORNELIA, born in 1750, was always his intimate

Influence of Frankfort companion. As the boy grew up, his native city exercised a very important influence upon his receptive mind. With the Seven Years' War came a whole line of new ideas. During the French occupation of Frankfort, Count THORANE was quartered in a part of the Goethe home. He was an art student, and kept several artists at work around him. Under his direction a French theater was set up, which aroused young Goethe's interest in theatrical representations, and in the effort to master the French language. The first cantos of KLOP-STOCK's *Messias,* and especially the Bible, were of the greatest influence in training his literary taste.

Education   His father gave personal supervision to his education, and tried to develop in him a habit of independent thinking, rather than to store his memory with facts. After receiving thus a many-sided, irregular, and **At Leipzig**   somewhat superficial education, he entered in 1765 the University of Leipzig, where he remained as a student of law until 1769. At first he attended regularly the lectures on law, but soon became more interested in others, especially those of Professor Gellert. Yet the dry and formal methods of teaching, which were prevalent, were unable to keep up his interest, and he soon found more delight in mixing in the society of "Little Paris," as the city was sometimes called, in attending the theater, or in traveling around at leisure. Now and then was composed some little poem; the two comedies, *Die Laune des Verliebten* (The Lover's Humor) and *Die Mit-schuldigen* (The Accomplices), date from this time. He turned his attention earnestly to art; the director of the art school assisting him to understand Winkleman's works and Lessing's Laokoon. A visit to the gallery in Dresden inspired him in this line, and opened up to him a new insight into art. He practiced much at drawing, in which he succeeded admirably.

A violent hemorrhage caused him to return home. His health was undermined, and during his long convalescence he associated much with a noble relative and friend of his mother's, CATHERINE VON KLETTENBERG, who had exercised a strong influence over him in his boyhood. He busied himself with reading, drawing, and performing experiments in alchemy, but paid very little attention to his profession.

At Strass-burg In order to bring his mind to the study of law his father sent him in 1770 to the University of Strassburg, where he remained a little over a year. Here also he paid little attention to his professional studies, but occupied himself with medicine and chemistry, and traveled much through the beautiful land of Alsace. Of great importance in his development was the circle of friends with whom he boarded. Among several who afterward became men of some note may be mentioned JUNG-STILLING[1] and HERDER; the latter, although only five years older, was far more advanced in experience and culture, and already a renowned writer. Through him he was led to study the old folksongs, Homer and Shakespeare. For Herder he took great delight in gathering the popular songs as he traveled through the country, and he frequently tried his own skill in imitating them. With Herder he read Goldsmith's *Vicar of Wakefield,* and soon afterward became intimately acquainted with just such a family as Goldsmith depicts. His love for the parson's daughter, FREDERIKE BRION, was the inspiration to many of the poems of this period. How delighted he was to make his trips to the little village of Sessenheim, to the north of Strassburg; how he became acquainted with her; what she was to him; how he finally left her, and could never forgive himself for it; how he never forgot her, who never forgot him, and who died, unmarried, in 1813—all this Goethe has portrayed in beautiful poetic fancy, yet in the main features truthfully, in *Dichtung und Wahrheit* (Poetry and Truth). Yet the best insight into his relations with Frederike can be seen from the numerous poems addressed to her, among which

---

[1]Stilling was the son of a poor charcoal burner. He worked his way up to be a country school-teacher, then a student of medicine, and later gained renown as an oculist. Still later he turned his attention to political economy, and became professor of that subject at the universities in Magdeburg and Heidelberg.

may be mentioned: *Hand in Hand und Lipp auf Lippe;
Es schlug mein Herz geschwind zu Pferde* (Welcome and
Departure) ; and best of all, the May-song, *Wie herrlich
leuchtet mir die Natur* (How gloriously beameth all nature
to me).

Notwithstanding the diversions and digressions from
his studies, he had paid enough attention to law to obtain
Graduation the degree of "Licentiate in Law" (not Doctor,
as he was called). Returning to Frankfort, he
was admitted to the bar, but paid little attention to the practice of his profession. More interesting and attractive to
him was the intercourse with friends of literary tastes.
Among these was the war minister, MERCK, a cultured, dis-
criminating critic, whose rare praise and candid censure
were important for Goethe's poetic development. Soon after
his return, a celebration in honor of Shakespeare was held
in Frankfort, and the young lawyer-poet was invited to de-
liver the oration. In this he expresses his ideas about poetry
in general, and protests against the French imitation of
Greek tragedy, and announces Shakespeare as his ideal. In
At Wetzlar the spring of 1772 Goethe went to Wetzlar
there to gain some practical experience at the
imperial supreme court. Thither he took the sketch of his
Götz, to which he now gave his attention. While there, he
was led to another of his youthful works, *Werther,* by his
attachment to CHARLOTTE BUFF. But as she was already
engaged to Kestner, one of Goethe's friends, he finally tore
himself away, and returned to Frankfort.

Soon after his return appeared his GÖTZ VON BERLICH-
INGEN, the incentive to which he received in Strassburg,
where he happened to read an autobiography of the gallant
knight with the iron hand.

According to history, Götz, a member of a family even yet
prominent in Würtemberg, went with his uncle Conrad to the
Imperial diet at Worms. Later he entered military service under

The Götz of history

several princes, and in one of his numerous campaigns, lost his right arm, which was replaced by one skillfully made from iron. In spite of the emperor's command for public peace, he continued his warfare, was then imprisoned, but soon set free, after which he lived quietly in his castle for two years, when the rebellious peasants compelled him to lead them. After the peasants were suppressed, he was accused of being a partaker in their insurrection, was long held a prisoner in Augsburg, was set free in 1530, on his promise to remain at his castle and not to seek revenge. He kept his promise, and only once more did he leave his home on military service, to accompany the emperor on a campaign against the Turks, and then against the French. He died at his castle, Hornberg, in 1562.

Goethe's Götz

In Goethe's drama the historical Götz and his time appear portrayed with genial power and originality; only the close of his life and many minor circumstances has the poet changed to suit his fancy.

In his castle lives GÖTZ, the man whom the princes hate, and to whom the oppressed turn for assistance, a knight who is subject to God, to the emperor, and to himself. He is in the company of his wife ELIZABETH, the most beautiful character of the piece, in whom the poet has woven the characteristics of his own mother, of his sister MARIA, who is intended to reflect the character of Frederike Brion, and of several comrades, among whom LERSE reminds us of the author's Strassburg friend of that name. The recently established imperial courts are offensive to him, and he will not adapt himself to the new order of things. His old heroic strength and his chivalrous spirit rise up within him, and lead him to struggle with the newly arisen powers. In this conflict the hero is almost ruined. Opposed to him stands ADALBERT VON WEISLINGEN, once his intimate companion, but now trying to satisfy his ambition by becoming a servile courtier. During one of his numerous quarrels, Götz succeeds in taking his former companion prisoner. His magnanimous treatment touches Weislingen's heart, and leads him to break the attachments to the court, and to rejoin his old friend. Their former bond of friendship is strengthened by Weislingen's engagement to Maria. Once more he is to go to the court to arrange his affairs, and the confiding Götz permits him to do so. This proves to be Weislingen's ruin, for to the intrigues of the court people, and to the heartless coquetry of ADELHEID VON WALLDORF, he is not equal. He deserts his friend and his betrothed, attaches himself to Götz's enemies, and marries Adelheid. Both of them now set out to ruin Götz, and influence the emperor to declare him an outlaw. The imperial troops surround his castle, and take him prisoner; but the emperor dismisses him on his promise to remain peacefully at his castle. Some time later, however, the rebellious peasants compel him to become their leader. After some hesitation, he consents to act in this capacity for four weeks, in the hope of being useful to the empire by checking the rage of the rebels. This gives Weislingen another chance at him. He succeeds in having him condemned to death, and is, furthermore, intrusted with the execution of the sentence. As Maria hears of this, she hastens to him, and begs him to spare her brother, and his own boyhood friend. He tears the sentence to pieces; yet it is all in vain, for the brave knight even now lies dying from his wounds. But his enemies, also, are destroyed,—Weislingen by poison which Adelheid has induced her paramour to give him, and Adelheid herself, convicted of adultery and murder, is condemned to death.

This production, rather a series of skillfully arranged scenes than a genuine drama, aroused Germany. Although the end does not agree with the historical facts, it is, nevertheless, a true picture of German manhood and German life in the era of the Reformation. It appeared at first without the name of the author, and when it was finally announced that the writer was Goethe, he became at once the greatest author and one of the most renowned men of Germany.

Of greater influence was the novel of Goethe's youth. DIE LEIDEN DES JUNGEN WERTHER (The Sorrows of Werther). This novel, which immediately gave its author an European renown is based on his experiences in Wetzlar. Soon after his arrival, CHARLOTTE BUFF made a deep impression on him. He called on her, and saw her in the surround-

ings of her luxurious and happy home. Before long he was
a daily guest; he romped with the boys of the family, told
stories to the girls, yet kept looking deeper into Lotte's eyes.
He did not change his conduct when he learned that her
heart was no longer free. The man to whom she had for
two years been engaged was KESTNER, an intimate friend
of Goethe's. He was some eight years older than Goethe,
a noble-hearted man, who had the utmost confidence in his
betrothed and in his friend. Goethe's relations to the young
lady were always upright and honorable; yet it is certain
that he became in love with her, but had the manhood to
tear himself away, and leave her and her lover undisturbed
in their devotion to each other. Not at once, however, did
he recover from his attachment, for pictures of Lotte were
long afterward hanging in his room, and he frequently
wrote to her and to Kestner.

Young JERUSALEM, whom he had known at Wetzlar, had
become weary of life, and shot himself. He had allowed
himself to fall desperately in love with a married woman
who, however, had character enough to reject all approaches.
Goethe was agitated by this news. He saw in Jerusalem
his own image, and in the object of Jerusalem's passion
he saw the picture of Lotte; he recognized to what he might
have been led, if he had not resisted the temptation in time.
The two principal characters of a romance stood before his
mind. The plan for this novel was further developed during
a trip to Wetzlar, which he made in the same year, when he
saw Lotte for the last time as a girl.

Thus *Werther's Leiden* became "fragments of a great
confession," as Goethe calls all his poetry. Yet Werther is
not Goethe. Werther perishes because he is wretched, and
is wretched because he is weak. Goethe was strong, was
master of himself; he saw the danger and evaded it; he tore
himself from the woman he loved instead of courting danger
by remaining near her. Yet much of Goethe lives in Wer-

8

ther, which may be seen from the incidents and language as well as from the character. It is that part which reappears under the mask of Weislingen, Clavigo, Faust, and other characters of his dramas, a part which we can not call the same figure in other dress, but which we all recognize as belonging to the same class; it is always a man of strong desire but of weak will power, an impressionable nature unable to attain self-mastery. Goethe was wavering because he was easily impressed, but his wavering was not due to weakness. He was tender-hearted, too. Hard-hearted sternness never was at his command, but resolution never failed him. Goethe kept the name of Lotte in his novel, and has made it renowned for all time, but Kestner, represented under the name of Albert, is treated as the husband of Lotte from the beginning. Naturally Kestner and Lotte were offended at being so mixed up in the affair of Jerusalem; but the poet finally succeeded in conciliating them, and they were long in friendly correspondence with him.

Such are the features at the bottom of the novel which startled Europe, and made for its author a world-wide reputation. Streams of tears were shed over it, not merely by youthful and sentimental souls, but by staid men and women; a violent Werther fever raged throughout Germany. Werther's costume, blue coat and yellow trousers, became the fashion among the young men. In spite of all the rage about the book, it was criticised severely. It may be said to be the outcome of the disease of the times, and not a struggle against it. It is filled with the spirit of the Storm and Stress period, and is so throughly permeated with the spirit of Rousseau, that we may almost say that if Rousseau's *La Nouvelle Héloise* had not appeared, *Werther's Leiden* would never have been written.

Other early work   Besides these important works of his youth numerous minor productions arose while he was at Frankfort, and *Faust* was begun at this time.

Although he was active in literature, he had by no means attained to a position in life such as his father had hoped he would. The visits of literary men, who were drawn to him by his new reputation, interrupted his work in law. Of especial importance was the visit of the two princes of Weimar in 1774.

In the spring of 1775, Goethe became betrothed to ANNA ELISABETH SCHONMANN, who is the LILI of many of his lyrics. The engagement was disapproved by both families, and Goethe himself did not find perfect satisfaction in it.

Swiss Journey
In order to get his mind off the matter, he decided to make a journey into Switzerland, to see, as he says, "whether I can get along without Lili." Yet among all the distraction of Switzerland, he could not free his mind from the charming girl at home; and on his return the old struggle was renewed, but the engagement was finally cancelled. He was free but not happy. His heart needed some one to love. He was much disturbed, and knew not what to do. As he was about to undertake a journey to Italy, an invitation came to spend a few weeks at the court of Weimar, as the guest of KARL AUGUST. Thither he went, arriving on Nov. 7, 1775.

First Two Decades in Weimar (1775-1794).

Court of Muses
The center and soul of the Weimar "Court of the Muses," was the widowed DUCHESS AMALIA, the sister of Frederick the Great, a vivacious and cultured woman. She was a widow at eighteen, and then for sixteen years was guardian of her sons and regent in the government. When Prince KARL AUGUST became eighteen, she turned the government over to him, and thereafter devoted herself to the cultivation of the fine arts, literature, music, and painting. Much like her was the young duke, whose teacher had been Wieland, and who now entered into a bond of friendship with Goethe, a friendship which was most intimate and happy during their long lives.

At first there reigned in the little court a wild and wanton life; unrestrained pleasures of all sorts, theatrical representations followed in rapid succession, and the **His position** soul of them all was the young poet-guest, who soon became more than a visitor. He was appointed privy councilor and later president of the chamber, the highest office the duke could give him. At the suggestion of Karl August he was ennobled by Emperor Joseph II. For a whole decade he managed the affairs of the government with complete devotion and faithfulness. He was at the same time director of the duke's private theater, wrote dramas for special occasions, drilled the court troupe, which consisted of all the gentlemen and ladies of the court, from the Duchess Amalia down, and played himself, both humorous and earnest pieces, with remarkable success. He was a frequent guest at the home of Herder. A warm friendship existed between him and the cultured and gifted FRAU VON STEIN, whose influence upon his poetic development was of great importance, and to whom many of his poems are dedicated. *Rastlose Liebe* (Restless Love), *Wanderers Nachtlied* (Wanderer's Night Song), and *Ueber allen Gipfeln* (Over All the Hilltops) may be mentioned as among the best. To the first ten years of his Weimar life belong also the beginnings of *Egmont, Torquato Tasso,* and *Wilhelm Meister*. *Iphigenie* was completed in prose in 1779, and played at the court with Goethe in the rôle of Orestes.

Swiss Journey In 1779 he and the duke took a trip to Switzerland. On the way they stopped at Strassburg, where he found Lili happy in her married life. While here he took a side trip to Sessenheim, the trip he had so often made ten years before. Here he was kindly received by Frederike and her people, and no word was uttered referring to their past relations, which would embarrass him. The description of the rest of his journey is well given in his *Letters from Switzerland,* addressed for the

most part to Frau von Stein. On their return trip they
stopped at Stuttgart, and were present at the New Year festivities of the military academy, where SCHILLER, twenty
years of age, with his head full of *Die Räuber,* saw the
author of *Götz* and *Werther.*

**Dissatisfac-
tion with
court duties**
But court life and official occupation could not
long satisfy the poet, for his poetic activity
seemed to be at a standstill, and his longing for
Italy became stronger and stronger. Finally he
decided to carry out the plans he had long secretly cherished. In September, 1786, Goethe went through Bavaria and
the Tyrol to Italy, where he remained nearly two years, for the
most part in Rome. Here he cast from him the last portions
of the Storm and Stress period of his life; his contemplation
of art and nature became clear, and rose to the highest of
ideals; and his poetic ability once more became aroused in
great activity. His *Italienische Reise* (Italian Journey) tells
us in detail about the experiences of these two important
years.

The first poetic fruit of this journey was IPHIGENIE AUF
TAURIS. While in Italy he rewrote it in iambic pentameters,
and it was published in 1787.

**Euripides's
Iphigenia**
The material is taken from the *Iphigenia in Tauris* of EURIPIDES, whose drama treats of the removal
of Diana's image from her temple in Tauris. When
the Greeks were ready to sail against Troy, they waited in vain
for favorable winds. Finally Agamemnon decides to sacrifice
his daughter IPHIGENIA, to appease the anger of the gods. Just
as the sacrificial knife is ready to fall, Diana relents, and carries
the girl away to barbarous Tauris, and establishes her as a
priestess in her temple, whose duty it is to sacrifice to the goddess the foreigners who land on the shores of Tauris. At the
command of Apollo, her brother ORESTES has murdered his
mother and her paramour, to avenge his father, whom they had
put to death. On account of this matricide, the Furies pursue
him night and day; but Apollo has promised him relief if he

will carry Diana's image away from her temple in Tauris. Accompanied by PYLADES, Orestes goes thither, and both are condemned to be sacrificed to the goddess by the hand of the priestess, who finally discovers her brother. All three succeed in carrying out a plan of escaping, and removing the image of Diana. TROAS, king of Tauris, who had consented to the purification of the image in sea water (the scheme they had adopted to get possession of the image), is greatly enraged when he discovers the deception, and starts to pursue the fugitives. Just here, however, Minerva stops him, and assures him that it is all in accordance with the will of the gods. Troas now bows in submission to the higher powers, and allows the fugitives to carry their image to Greece.

Goethe's Iphigenie   The German poet has replaced this external solution by an internal one, which is the fruit of the Christian spirit. The heroine brings about the solution; she is transformed, under Goethe's pen, from a pagan to a Christian woman whose character is resplendently fair. While in her own home sin and crime have been continually increasing, she has remained pure in this wild land of Tauris, has won the barbarians from their sacrifices of strangers, and has scattered blessings around her. TROAS, impressed by her moral and self-sacrificing nature, falls in love with her. After she has gently and repeatedly rejected his wooing, he commands her to resume the sacrifices of strangers to the goddess, and sends her two who have recently been found, and who prove to be her brother ORESTES and his friend PYLADES. They have come, at the command of Apollo, to await a hand of help in the temple of his sister, and to be forgiven for the crime of matricide by bringing his sister away from the temple. This they interpret to mean the image of Diana. Brother and sister recognize each other, and by confessing to her his guilt, Orestes is freed from the curse that has been resting upon him, and the Furies leave. Now they plan to deceive TROAS; IPHIGENIA is to represent to the king that the image of Diana has been desecrated by the presence of one who has been persecuted by the Furies, and must be purified by sea water before the victims can be sacrificed. Once at the seacoast, they could escape to a concealed vessel, and then make their way home. Iphigenia's pure soul is troubled on account of

the deception she is to practice, and after struggling for some
time, she conquers her doubts, and confesses the whole matter to
the king. Troas is completely overcome when ORESTES finally
recognizes the true meaning of Apollo's command to be to bring
his own sister instead of the image of Apollo's sister from Tauris
to Greece. Then the king allows them to go. Iphigenia's pure
and noble mind had overcome him, and her mild, reconciling
words at their departure lead him to utter a farewell greeting.

The reception of this piece at home was cool—the people
had expected a fiery, stormy piece like *Götz,* and were disappointed. Even his intimate friends, Herder in the lead,
were not satisfied; time alone has given to the drama the
recognition it deserves.

EGMONT (1788), which he had planned twelve years before in Frankfort, was also completed in Italy, but remained
in prose.

Historical Egmont
The material is taken from the struggle of the Netherlands against Spanish rule. The historical EGMONT,
a descendant of an old family of the Netherlands,
was the idol of the people. He had won a reputation as a warrior,
had occupied high positions under the king, and had confidence
in his sovereign. King Philip II of Spain determined to subju-
gate this largely Protestant country, and increase the Catholic
influence there. To accomplish this, he sent the Duke of Alva
with a large army. Egmont, who had his people's welfare at
heart, and in whom they were trusting for help, was secretly
entrapped, given a mock trial, and finally executed.

Goethe's Egmont
Unlike the historical Egmont, the hero of the drama
is a joyful, amiable leader of the people, who turns
from his earnest thoughts and occupations to CLARA,
a girl from among the people, and finally is led, through his own
carelessness, into the trap set for him by the DUKE OF ALVA. He
is imprisoned and then executed. Clara, who has tried in vain to
arouse the people to do something to save him, drinks poison in
the presence of the "good BRAKENBURG," her faithful lover.
Shortly before his death, a vision reveals to him the form of
Clara hovering upon a cloud; as the goddess of liberty she announces the victory of the fatherland in the struggle, in which
his life is the first to be sacrificed.

Egmont has been much criticised. It can scarcely be called a drama; it is rather a series of masterly scenes, from which we see an important time with its characters passing rapidly before us, and into which there is woven a charming love-idyl. In spite of all criticism it has remained a favorite with the public.

The poet was happy in Italy, and his stay there was several times prolonged. When he finally arrived at Weimar, he was honorably received by the court and by society. The position which the duke offered him was attractive; it was that of a friend whose only duties should be those he wished to lay upon himself. In spite of all these circumstances, he could not become perfectly satisfied in his German surroundings. To German nature, German art, German life and faith, he had become a stranger; his heart longed for Italy, for southern nature, and ancient art. This longing led him to complete his TORQUATO TASSO, two acts of which he had taken to Rome with him in prose; there he began to rewrite it in verse, completed it in Weimar, and published it in 1789.

TORQUATO TASSO (1544-95) hands his epic poem, *Jerusalem Delivered*, to DUKE ALFONSO of Ferrara, whose sister, LEONORO crowns the poet with a laurel wreath. Just then ANTONIO appears, the duke's minister who has returned from a mission to the pope. He can not refrain from ridiculing the act which arouses his jealousy. Tasso attempts to win the diplomat for his friend, but fails. Their hatred increases until one day Tasso challenges his enemy to a duel. The duke, who finds them thus occupied, punishes the poet as mildly as possible by confining him to his room. He chides Antonio, also, and soon commands him to liberate Tasso, and try to win his confidence. He tries it, but Tasso is so imbittered and excited, that he imagines everyone is treating him falsely, and as a proof of friendship, he bids Antonio ask the duke's permission for him to leave Ferrara. Regretfully, but graciously, the duke grants the permission, in the hope of curing him. But when the hour of separation from the princess comes, he allows himself to be carried away, and to confess his long-concealed love for her. Repulsed by the princess, forsaken by all, there remains for him only the strong character of Antonio, to whom he now attaches himself, and rises to strong manhood.

In this drama, poor in action, but rich in inner life and unsurpassed in the delineation of character, there is mirrored the first decade of Goethe's Weimar life; especially the incongruity between the poetic spirit and the court spirit, under which both German and Italian poets had to suffer, and the discord in his own breast between the poet and the statesman, from which Goethe by this piece wished to free himself.

While walking one day, soon after his return from Italy, he was accosted by a sprightly young girl, CHRISTIANE VUL-PIUS, who handed him a petition in behalf of her brother. He was attracted by her appearance, visited her often, and she helped him arrange his work on botany. Soon he took her to his home, and from that time she was regarded as his wife, although not formally married until 1806.

French Revolution   The French Revolution annoyed him much, and the two little plays which were called out by it were written in a derisive tone, and are unworthy of the pen of Goethe. In 1792 he accompanied the duke on his expedition against the French, and has described his experiences in his *Campagne in Frankreich*. When the news of the execution of Louis XVI came, in order to take his attention away from the atrocities across the Rhine, he went to work on the old legend of *Reineke Fuchs*. The result of this labor is his poem of the same title, written in hexameters and composed of twelve cantos. In the meantime the duke had given to his friend the house which was his home for fifty years. From the time of Goethe's death until 1885, the house remained closed; at this time, with its valuable collections, its library, and much of its furniture

it was presented to the state, and opened to the public as a
GOETHE-NATIONAL MUSEUM.

Longing for Italy After his return from Italy, Goethe was no longer the society man that he had been before; he
lived almost alone; WIELAND and HERDER had
become estranged from him; and society never recovered
from its revulsion at his relation to Christiane Vulpius.
SCHILLER, whom he found at Weimar on his return, and
whom he was influential in sending to Jena as professor, did
not become his friend; and for six years the two poets
worked side by side, and yet alone, without understanding
each other, and without being able to become intimate
Friendship with Schiller friends. But in the spring of 1794 something
brought them together, and the time of a new
spring dawned for them both. Yet before we
consider the bond of friendship and their eleven years of
intimate relation in literary work, we must look at SCHILLER,
his early life, and his development.

FRIEDRICH VON SCHILLER (1759-1805).

His Youth and Early Writings (1759-1784).

JOHANN CHRISTOPH FRIEDRICH SCHILLER was born on
Nov. 10, 1759, in the little town of Marbach in Würtemberg.
His grandfather and great-grandfather had been bakers, and
Parentage his father was a lieutenant who gradually rose
to be captain, and as such he was stationed for
some time in Lorch, where his son received his first formal
instruction from Pastor MOSER, whom he has immortalized in
Die Räuber. His mother was a landlord's daughter, a pious
and thoughtful woman, who exercised a lasting influence
upon her son.

In 1766 the family moved to Ludwigsburg, where the
boy attended the Latin school. He expected to enter a monastery, and passed the necessary examinations for admission. His plans were suddenly interrupted by DUKE KARL

FRIEDRICH VON SCHILLER

THE GOETHE MONUMENT AT VIENNA

EUGEN, who had recently established a military
At the academy academy for the education of officers' sons who
wished to prepare for the army, for law, or for
medicine. Although Schiller and his father objected, young
Friedrich was obliged to give up the desire to study theology,
enter the academy, and begin the study of law.

Two years later the school was transferred to Stuttgart,
a department of medicine was added, and Schiller decided
to take up that study, not so much from a love for the profession, as from a desire to be free from the disagreeable
study of law. The curriculum furnished him with a fair
knowledge of the classics, but this knowledge was widened
by extensive private reading. Although modern authors
were forbidden, he managed to keep well posted on what
was going on in the literary world. Among the
Literary influences writings that especially interested him were
Luther's hymns, and Klopstock's odes and *Mes-
sias*. His first acquaintance with SHAKESPEARE was a marked
event in his career; but the author who influenced him
most was ROUSSEAU, whose glowing pictures of nature filled
his imagination, and whose scorn for despotism and conven-
tionality was practically impressed on the boy's mind by
what he saw around him. Finally came the productions of
the Storm and Stress period, first of all *Götz* and *Werther*.
KLINGER and SCHUBART were his models, and the Storm and
Stress spirit is prominent in all his early poems.

DIE RÄUBER (The Robbers), the greatest and best of his
early writings, begun when he was eighteen years old, and
printed in 1781, was first played at Mannheim. The author
intended it to represent contemporary affairs, but when it
was first presented, for fear of arousing too much opposition, it was made to represent the times of the sixteenth century.

The ruling COUNT VON MOOR has two sons, KARL and FRANZ.
Karl is a student at Leipzig, Franz lives with his father in the

castle. Karl the elder, of noble and energetic, yet unrestrained
and unrefined disposition, has allowed himself to be carried into
all sorts of dissipation at the university, which he confesses to
his father in a letter full of repentance. He begs for forgive-
ness, and wishes to return home, there to begin life anew with
AMALIA, who has cherished a tender love for him during his
absence. But Franz, a man ugly in physique and villainous in
heart, who has long wished to cheat his brother out of his inheritance and attract to himself the heart of his brother's betrothed, writes a false letter, in which a Leipzig friend informs
the father that Karl has committed numerous crimes, and is
under warrant for arrest. The old man believes it, and though
his heart still wavers, he finally yields to the influence of Franz,
and instructs him to write the brother that he is disinherited
forever. This drives him to despair, and he becomes the leader
of a wild, reckless band of men, who go to the forests of Bohemia, and there lead desperate lives. They persecute the vicious, chastise those in high positions, sell to the highest bidders
the offices and positions of honor, and turn the patriots out of
their houses—in short, they try to cure the unjust world with
fire and sword. In the meantime, Franz has completed his measure of horrors, and has cast his father into a dungeon. He is
now master, and rules like a tyrant. Everybody and everything
bow before him, except Amalia, who rejects his wooing, although she rather believes that Karl was killed in the army.
Karl's conscience finally awakens, and a longing drives him
homeward. He discovers his father, but the old man dies when
he learns who has set him at liberty. Franz commits suicide
when the robber band attacks his castle at night. But Karl
himself can not marry Amalia, who has been faithful to him so
long, because he had once promised the band never to leave
them. She begs him to kill her, which he does, and then gives
himself up to justice.

Estimate This drama, born right from the Storm and
Stress spirit, displays all the weaknesses and ex-
travagances of the time. Yet in spite of all its unnatural-
ness and exaggeration, it is far superior to most pieces of
this epoch. Before its publication Schiller was an unknown,

subordinate army surgeon; a short time after it appeared, he was celebrated throughout Germany. The piece was in harmony with the revolutionary spirit of the time, and it had an active influence on the youth of the country. On the other hand, criticism was abundant; but no one has criticised it more sharply than the author himself, who wrote, a few years afterward, as follows: "If I should pick out the most appropriate criticism, it would be that I attempted to delineate men two years before I had a chance to learn what men are."

Flight from Stuttgart Schiller's presence at the first representation of his drama was kept very quiet, and the duke paid no attention to the play until a copy of a severe criticism was handed him. Since the poet had gone to Mannheim without permission, a second time, the duke forbade him all intercourse with foreigners, and commanded him never to write comedy or anything of the kind again. After a written request to be relieved from such a command, had been returned to him unopened, he withdrew from his oppressive circumstances, by fleeing to Mannheim. He had had great hopes of assistance from the theater manager, DALBERG, but he was doomed to disappointment. For fear of offending the Duke of Würtemberg, Dalberg was distant and reserved, and refused to advance money for *Fiesco,* which Schiller had brought with him. For fear of being turned over to the Duke of Würtemberg, he withdrew to a small village near Mannheim, and again, because he thought that he was not safe there, he accepted an invitation of FRAU VON WOLZOGEN, with whose son he had been acquainted in the academy, to Bauerbach near Meiningen, obtaining the money for traveling expenses from the sale of his second drama.

At Bauerbach Six happy months he spent in this country retreat, in the company of his hostess, and more especially of her sixteen-year-old daughter, who many a time figured in the young man's mind as the future wife of a great poet. He established an intimate friendship with Librarian REINWALD, who later became his brother-in-law, and who provided him with all the books he could use. Here he completed *Louise Millerin* which he had begun in Stuttgart, and developed his plan for *Don Carlos*. In the meantime, Dalberg had learned of the new piece, and had entered into a correspondence which ended in calling Schiller to Mannheim as director of the theater.

With FIESCO (1784), first played in Mannheim, the author enters upon the realm of history, the field in which his later and grander dramas were so successful.

The Genoese republic attained to the height of its power under ANDREAS DORIA, whose energy had brought to the state a high degree of prosperity and contentment. Quite different, however, was his nephew, GIANETTINO, whose only motive was his own selfish ambition. Destined to become his uncle's successor, he ridiculed the rights of individuals and the laws of the republic, and was working in every possible way to gain the rank of a duke. He was hated throughout the city. In opposition to this tyranny, there was formed a conspiracy whose leader was FIESCO. Carefully concealing his own ambitious plans, he was skillful enough to attract the nobility to him by his magnanimous hospitality, and to win the hearts of the people by pretending to be an advocate of their rights. To conceal from the Dorias his real character, he kept up an intimate relation with Gianettino, and pretended to be in love with his sister. In the meantime, however, he was secretly negotiating with foreign powers. VERRINA, one of the leading conspirators, an unflinching republican patriot, discovers Fiesco's purpose, and resolves to save the state from such a fate. Yet Fiesco goes on with his preparations, and, under one pretext and another, he brings a vessel into the harbor, and fills the city with disguised soldiers. After thwarting several attempts against his life and that of his wife, and in spite of the betrayal of his plans to his mortal enemy,—in which attempts and betrayal a vicious MOOR plays an important part, —he sees himself on the point of reaching his goal—becoming Duke of Genoa. Just at this point the avenging hand of Verrina reaches him, and plunges him into the sea.

This piece is also the product of the Storm and Stress period; as the first drama was a tirade against the corruption of the world in general, *Fiesco* storms against the old conventional forms of government, and represents the republican ideas of which the times were full.

KABALE UND LIEBE (Intrigue and Love, 1784), the title by which *Louise Millerin* is better known, was of much greater influence. It throws a bright light on the society of the despotic little states of Germany at a time when the upper classes thought that they had a perfect right to trample the common people underfoot.

Major FERDINAND VON WALTER is destined by his father, the president at the residence of a prince, to become the husband of a deserted mistress of the prince. But his heart has chosen otherwise, he loves LOUISA MILLER, the daughter of the town musician, and in spite of prejudices and in spite of his father's plans, he is determined to marry her. But love is overcome by intrigue. Since the president can not bring his son to voluntary obedience, he plans to separate the lovers by a vicious scheme. At his command Louisa's father and mother are thrown into the tower; his secretary WURM, a cunning villain, by representing to Louisa that a death sentence is about to be pronounced upon her father, influences her to write at his dictation a love letter to a frivolous courtier. The letter is at once put where Ferdinand finds it. Since Louisa has promised to keep silent, and must confess that she has written the letter, Ferdinand, with remarkable stupidity, falls into the trap, loses faith in his loved one, gives up in despair, and poisons her as well as himself. When on the point of death, he learns the truth from the lips of his loved one dying before him.

Estimate   Although this piece is full of much that is improbable and extravagant, in spite of Goethe's just criticism, that it testifies to the unusual genius rather than to the broad and ripe culture of the author, it marks a great advance on the other two pieces; especially in the characterization of some of the individuals. The picture of the despotism of the petty state is rough, now and then over-drawn, but on the whole, true. The dramatic element is very important, and is just as effective to-day as ever.

Introduction to Karl August
In the same year, the poet had the privilege of reading the first act of his *Don Carlos* to Karl August, who, visiting in Mannheim, honored him with the title of Councilor to the Duke of Weimar. Seeing that his high ideals were not comprehended, and that he was not supported in them by the actors, he began to long to get away from Mannheim. In June of this year, there came to him from Leipsig a handsome letter case, containing four portraits, a letter full of admiration for his writings, and one of his poems set to music. Schiller was never more touched than he was by this tribute of love and respect, and although for some reason he did not answer it for nearly six months, there did develop from it a corres-pondence which led to a gratifying and important friendship.

Invitation to Leipzig
The leader of the little band of admirers lived at Dresden; this was KÖRNER, the father of the poet, THEODOR KÖRNER. Led on by the invita-tion of these friends, Schiller went to Leipsig in April, 1785.

Second Poetic Period (1785-1794).

During his first summer in Saxony, the poet lived at Gohlis, a village near Leipsig, in a little house which is still shown to his admirers as the place where he wrote the *Lied an die Freude* (Hymn to Joy).

At Dresden
A longing for Körner's society led him to Dres-den, where he found this friend, a man of strong character and true culture, whose influence proved helpful to him both in his life and in his writings. Almost two years were spent in quiet seclusion at Körner's vineyard country seat in Loschwitz, where the poet worked industriously at *Don Carlos*.

DON CARLOS (1787), composed in iambic pentameters

after Lessing's example, marks the transition from Schiller's youthful dramas to the five great dramas of his maturity. After many changes during the four years in which it was being composed, the titular hero gradually gave place to Marquis Posa, the representative of the poet's cosmopolitan ideas; from the original intention of portraying the gloomy family of Philip II, the author passed to a didactic drama which was to proclaim ideas of universal liberty and toleration. This poetic message of freedom, appearing as it did two years before the French Revolution, was enthusiastically received by young Germany.

DON CARLOS loves his stepmother, ELIZABETH OF VALOIS, who had been destined to him, and who is yet devoted to him. Thus the family life is thoroughly unhappy; the king regards his wife and son with suspicion and jealousy, while they are consumed with anger against the man who has made them unhappy. The bitterness of their position is increased by the king's confessor and the DUKE OF ALVA, who watch them closely, and take every opportunity to arouse the king against them. The infante's friend, MARQUIS POSA, after long absence returns from Brussels, with his heart full of desires for the liberation of the Netherlands. Through his influence the infante meets the queen, who induces him to ask from his father the command of the troops destined to Flanders, thereby hoping to lead him from his brooding to a life of activity. KING PHILIP, however, refuses to grant the request, saying that a man and not a boy is needed, and announces the Duke of Alva as the man for the mission. He is surprised at receiving a letter, which he supposes to come from the queen, inviting him to an interview. He is much disappointed when he finds the author to be the PRINCESS EBOLI, a court lady who has long loved him. When he replies coolly to her hints of love, she at once surmises whom he loves, and decides to take revenge by informing the king. In connection with Alva and the confessor, she completes her revenge by stealing some letters, from the infante to the queen, and giving them to the king. The latter is beside himself, and prays for a man to help him in his extremity. This man is Marquis Posa, who now becomes the hero of the drama. The king gives him

9

his confidence, and listens to his speeches about cosmopolitan
freedom and public benefaction. He takes the man into his
service, gives him the most influential position at court, and even
commissions him to search out the heart of the queen. The marquis takes advantage of his high position to intrigue secretly
against the king. According to his plan, Don Carlos was quietly
to withdraw to the Netherlands, and from Brussels, in combina-
tion with Egmont and Orange, to make the Spanish throne trem-
ble. The queen was to arouse the infante's enthusiasm for the
undertaking. To shield more thoroughly his friend from suspicion, and to help him away from the court, Posa sacrifices himself, by pretending that he is the one who really loves the queen.
This, however, leads to his being shot, and does not help his
friend. Don Carlos, too, is ruined; while saying farewell to the
queen before his departure for the Netherlands, he is surprised
by his father, and at once turned over as a prisoner.

The desire for a settled position, for which Karl August's
repeated encouragement led him to hope, induced him to go
to the ducal residence. On his arrival in the
Visit to Weimar summer of 1787, he found Goethe absent in Italy,
and friendly relations with Herder and Wieland
were slow in developing. He continued the study of history
which he had begun in Dresden, and in December went to
Meiningen to visit his sister, who had married Reinwald,
and his friend Frau von Wolzogen. With her son, his former schoolmate, he rode to Rudolstadt, to renew the acquaintance of FRAU VON LENGEFELD and her two daughters,
CAROLINE and CHARLOTTE, whom he had met in Mannheim.
He was so happy and contented in the circle of these amiable
and intelligent ladies that he found it hard to return to
Weimar. That he might enjoy more of their society, he
moved in May, 1788, to the little village of Volkstedt, a half-
hour's walk from Rudolstadt. Here he worked
At Volkstedt hard on his *Geschichte des Abfalls der vereinig-
ten Niederlande* (History of the Revolt of the
Netherlands), and read to the Misses Lengefeld the separate

chapters as they were finished. In July this work came to a temporary conclusion, and was never completed; the fragment breaking off with the founding of Alva's rule (1567).

At the same time he occupied himself with classical antiquities, and became so wrapped up in his studies that a passion for the golden age of Greek mythology took possession of him. To this he gave expression in his poem, *Die Götter Griechenlands* (The Gods of Greece), which laments the decay of the Greek polytheism. To this same line of study is due the rich didactic poem, *Die Künstler* (The Artists), in which he wished to show the value of art in the development of man. At Charlotte's request he translated the *Iphigenia in Aulis* of Euripides.

Greek influence

On Goethe's recommendation he was appointed as extraordinary professor of history in the university of Jena, where he began his lectures in 1789. Soon after this he became engaged to CHARLOTTE VON LENGEFELD, and in February they were married at Wenigen-Jena. Enjoying his home to the fullest extent, he now worked with renewed zeal and energy. Besides his lectures he began to write the *Geschichte des dreizigjährigen Krieges* (History of the Thirty Years' War), in which only the first half of the war is fully treated—to Wallenstein's death. This fills the first four books, while the fifth sums up the events as far as the Peace of Westphalia. The characteristic of this work is brilliant and sublime representation; and the liveliness of tone and style—heretofore unknown in German history writing—won many advocates to the study of history.

Call to Jena

But Schiller was not equal to such exertions, and in the winter of 1790 he was seized with a catarrhal fever, leading to a chest disease, from which he never wholly recovered. In the following year he was compelled to give up all his work. A sojourn at Carlsbad brought him some relief, but completely exhausted his means. Two patrons, however, came to his relief with an annuity of about $750, to be extended through three years.

Study of philosophy

Schiller now turned his attention to Kant's philosophy, and as a result of this study we have a series of stimulating and instructive philosophical and æsthetical essays: *Ueber Anmuth und Würde* (Grace and Dignity); *Ueber naive und sentimentalische Dichtung* (Naive and Sentimental Poetry). In the latter he compares and points out the difference between ancient and modern poetry, between the classic and romantic elements. The naive poet is natural; the sentimental poet seeks to be so. The former reproduces reality; the latter represents the ideal. *Ueber die ästhetische Erziehung des Menschen* (Æsthetic Education of Man) discusses in twenty-seven letters, the cultivating power and influence of beauty on human life, both in particular and in general.

Visit to boyhood home

Being free from financial anxiety, he was enabled to visit the home of his childhood. For nearly a year he and his wife remained in southern Germany, first at Heilbronn, then, since the duke was so gracious as not to notice his presence, at Ludwigsburg; later, after the duke's death, he went to Stuttgart. Here he formed an important and profitable acquaintance with the publisher COTTA. They decided to establish an artistic and literary periodical, *Die Horen,* in editing which the leading writers, especially Goethe, should be induced to take part. To carry out this undertaking, Schiller returned to Jena in May, 1794. Goethe, who had already promised his co-operation, soon came to consult Schiller about the matter, and at this time

Intimacy with Goethe

the gap that had so long existed between them disappeared. Rapidly were they drawn together in a friendship which was broken only by Schiller's death in 1805. It was a bond of friendship and a partnership of poets, the like of which has seldom been seen in history.

Goethe's and Schiller's Co-operation (1794-1805).

The announcement of the HOREN under Schiller's management, met with favor throughout Germany. It was the purpose to treat all subjects that could be discussed with taste and with the philosophical spirit, and it should also be open to philosophical problems as well as to poetical and historical productions. The greatest men of Germany promised their support in the editorial department, but most of them sent nothing at all, and the others sent things of minor importance. Even Goethe contributed only unimportant writings. But the *Horen* which existed until 1797 had been not only the cause of Goethe's and Schiller's living and working together, but also the means of leading Schiller once **Schiller's** more to poetry, although not one of his dramas, **return to** and only a few of his minor poems, appeared **poetry** in it. His return to his first love was completed by his reading Goethe's *Wilhelm Meister.* He wrote Goethe, "The poet is the only true man, and the best philosopher is only a caricature of him."

Fully twenty years before, Goethe had planned his romance, WILHELM MEISTER'S LEHRJAHRE (Apprenticeship); the first scenes were written before the Italian journey, but the whole was not finished until 1796.

WILHELM MEISTER, the son of a rich merchant, after youthful indulgences, sets out to follow his father's calling. He is scarcely under way when an old mania once more becomes master of him. He loses all interest in the business calling, and travels for some time with a band of actors. Among the characters he meets, the most interesting are the HARP-PLAYER and MIGNON, with their beautiful songs (among others, "Know'st Thou the Land where the Fair Citron Blooms," "The Minstrel"). In company with the actors, he now comes to a castle, where for the first time he meets cultured and aristocratic society, into whose manners he tries to train himself. A great influence is exerted upon him by LOTHARIO, whom he regards as the ideal of cultured manhood, and whose sister he marries.

This novel portrays life just as it is in bare reality; and although it can not be called immoral, yet it does arouse a moral dissatisfaction which is by no means amended in the development of the hero.

In addition to the *Horen,* which was devoted mainly to prose work, Schiller began the publication of the *Müsenalmanach* (Muses' Calendar), which was to be devoted to poetry. The principal contributors were Goethe and Schiller, and in the first two volumes appeared a number of their most beautiful poems; among others Schiller's *Die Macht des Gesangs* (The Power of Song), *Die Ideale* (Ideal and Life), telling how life may be brightened by high ideals, *Würde der Frauen* (Dignity of Women); woman's moral beauty must harmonize the harsh and hateful in life; and the excellent poem in which he allegorically compares poetry to an unknown maiden, *Das Madchen aus der Fremde.*

But the most striking thing in the *Musenalmanach* was the well-known series of epigrams which, under the name of *Xenien,* the two poets sent out like flashes of lightning against their literary enemies, and against what they regarded as faulty in literature. Some of them, however, were friendly greetings to those who were in sympathy with them.

Soon the two great poets felt themselves called on to work at something grander and better. After a pause of nine years Schiller once more returned to the drama, and in 1796 began his Wallenstein. While he was occupied in the preparations for this work, Goethe had completed HERMANN UND DOROTHEA (1797).

French Revolution the background

The year in which this poem was written was one of anxiety in Germany, and was one of the most eventful in the French Revolution. Naturally enough Goethe's mind was occupied by the agitations going on around him; and some four years before, he had accompanied the duke on his campaign to France, where experience taught him the hardships of war. His observations during this trip proved to be profitable to him when he came to write *Hermann und Dorothea;* and many an incident is based on what he saw during his life in camp. The whole picture of the Revolution, however, was before his mind, and the numerous scenes, suggested by those exciting years, can not be limited to any one period. The thread of the plot and several of the characters were suggested by circumstances nearer at home. In the fall of 1795 French emigrants, who had fled to Würzburg, and who were driven from there by the bishop, became scattered through the country around Eisenach and Weimar. These emigrants reminded the author of the Lutherans, who, three quarters of a century before, had been driven from Salzburg, to immigrate to the districts of Prussia, a thousand miles from home. Upon looking through the reports about these wanderers, he found the following story:

Story of Salzburg emigrants "In Altmühl, a town of Bavaria, a well-to-do citizen had in vain urged his son to marry. As the Salzburg emigrants were passing through the town, this young man took a fancy to a young woman in their midst, and determined to marry her. On inquiring, he found that she was from an honest family, and had always conducted herself well, but differing from her parents in religion, she had been compelled to leave them. He then went to his father, and told him that he was ready to marry, provided he could have the emigrant maiden. His father was surprised, and attempted to dissuade him from his project. Some friends and the parson were called in to help persuade the youth to give up his purpose; but it was all in vain. The pastor finally took the young man's side, and argued that it might all be in accordance with the will of Providence, and that it might be the very best thing for the youth; and they at last gave their consent. He then went straightway to the girl, and asked her how she liked it in this land. Her reply was, 'Very well.' Then he asked how she would like to become a servant in his father's home. Once more she answered, 'Very willingly.' After telling him what she could do, and assuring him that she would be faithful, he took her home and presented her to his father, who at once asked if she were willing to marry his son. She replied that they should not tease her, that she had been hired as a servant, and that she expected to earn well her bread. When the father and the son also showed that they were in earnest, she declared that she would be content."

This story gave Goethe the germ of his poem, and in it he found his leading characters, except the mother and the apothecary. At first his purpose was to keep the poem in narrow limits, but it grew to a length of 2,000 hexameters, **Dedication** divided into nine cantos, each of which is dedicated to one of the nine muses. The scene is changed, it is no longer the story of fugitives of a bygone age, but it is a mirror in which are reflected the movements and changes of the great revolution, so familiar to the minds of the German people. The poem is among the most powerful as well as the most charming of the poet's great works. It is merely a love story of the most humble kind, except as the characters are transfigured by their connection with the French Revolution. It is the product of a free and easy artistic effort, and can be thoroughly enjoyed without much in the way of introduction and commentary. It is the only one of the author's greater works that he took real delight in reading in his old age. For much of the impulse to write the poem Goethe acknowledges his indebtedness to Voss, whose *Luise* was so attractive to him that he committed large portions to memory.

In the spring of 1797 Schiller purchased a garden and summer house in Jena, from which he had a beautiful view of the Saale Valley. Here during the summer of the same years he produced many of his charming ballads, among them the following: *Der Taucher* (The Diver), *Der Handschuh* (The Glove), *Der Ring des Polykrates* (The Ring of Polykrates), *Ritter Toggenburg* (The Knight Toggenburg), *Der Gang nach dem Eisenhammer* (The Walk to the Forge).

Within a few years afterward appeared also the following excellent poems of the same kind: *Kampf mit dem Drachen* (Fight with the Dragon), *Hero und Leander, Kassandra,* and *Der Graf von Hapsburg.* During the same time and much in emulation with Schiller, Goethe produced in this same class of poetry the following: *Der Zauberlehrling* (The Pupil in Magic), *Die Braut von Korinth, Schäfers Klagelied* (The Shepherd's Lament), *Nachtgesang* (Night Song), and *Trost in Thränen* (Comfort in Tears).

While occupied with these ballads, Schiller's mind was also engaged in developing the piece that may be called the crown of his lyric and didactic poetry. It was DAS LIED VON DER GLOCKE (Song of the Bell). The author received his first impulse to write it when visiting a bell foundry at Rudolstadt in 1788. He went there frequently, and became familiar with the art of bell-casting, and expected to put such knowledge to use in writing the poem at once, but it was not completed until 1800, and at that time formed the main article in the *Musenalmanach.* It is composed of two parts, moving in parallel lines: one describes the manual processes in casting a bell, accompanied by the words of the master founder; the other is devoted to the writer's own reflections on human life, arranged in beautiful pictures and touching upon all the circumstances of individual life—childhood, youth, love, marriage, home, and destiny, and then proceeding to the community and state in their various conditions. These reflections are made at each step in the mechanical process, are suggested and introduced by the same, and have a connection with each other just as the various stages in the casting have.

While busy writing these smaller poems, Schiller was working at Wallenstein (1799). Since the hero of this the author's greatest drama, is one of the foremost characters in German history, let us consider for a moment the historical Wallenstein before we go to the one created by Schiller.

Historical Wallenstein WALLENSTEIN was born in Bohemia in 1583, of poor Protestant parents, but was sent to a Jesuit college, where he was converted to Catholicism. A wonderful story is told of his falling from a third story window and receiving no injuries, and of his becoming a fervent religious man, because the Madonna had saved him from harm in the fall. He inherited from his first wife considerable property, and another inheritance from an uncle made him a wealthy man. Through his influence and his military services at the outbreak of the Thirty Years' War, he gained the favor of the emperor, and was allowed to buy up large tracts of confiscated land at a nominal price. Among these he secured the princely estate of Friedland, and later on was made a duke. He became the commander-in-chief of the imperial forces. Horrible deeds were done by his troops; he became the scourge of the land, and drew the curses of all Europe down upon him. At the diet of Ratisbon the storm burst, and the emperor sacrificed him to his enemies. From this time he was a different man, wavering and unsocial, suspicious, gloomy, and restless. He turned his attention to astrology, and tried to gain from the stars strength for his wavering mind. The emperor came into sore need, and reinstated the fallen general, not from favor or good will, but because no one else was equal to raising an army. Wallenstein now used his authority for the accomplishment of his own ends. He negotiated with the Swedes, first merely to increase his power; this negotiation led him to think of the tremendous act of treason, without any serious thought of carrying it out. He gave his confidence to OCTAVIO PICCOLOMINI, who had been sent by the court to watch him and to betray him. Secret plans were set in motion to remove him from his command, and his enemies tried to detach his army from him. He hastened his negotiations with the Swedes, but just as he made up his mind to go over to them, and before his intention could be carried out, he was killed by assassins who thought they were acting in accordance with the emperor's will.

Schiller's Wallenstein Choosing as his hero this powerful and picturesque figure of the Thirty Years' War, Schiller has reproduced those times of terror. The drama begins with events near the close of Wallenstein's life, and instead of remaining within the confines of a single play, it developed into a trilogy divided as follows:

WALLENSTEIN'S LAGER (Camp). In this the hero, the spirit of the whole, does not appear at all. It gives a clear picture of the wild soldier life, and at the same time shows the real roots of the general's power. In the individual soldiers is reflected the army and the commander to whom they are all perfectly devoted. Several other characters besides soldiers are woven into the "Lager," and they are all true to life. Although many elements are here brought together, one spirit holds them as by magic; for Wallenstein they will live or die; and when they hear that the emperor is on the point of disbanding their army, they all object; neither power nor artifice can separate them from their father.

DIE PICCOLOMINI. This part, in five acts, presents us the hero, who has perfect confidence in the army which he has created and with which he expects to make himself master of Germany. He is anxious for the crown of Bohemia, which he can obtain only by an alliance with the Swedes. He hesitates to turn traitor, and waits for some decisive action of the stars. To remove him from his inaction, two of his officers, ILLO and TERZKY, resort to deception. By interpolation they obtain the signatures of all the generals, pledging themselves to remain obedient and true to their commander, even if he should desert the emperor. One of them notices the deception—it is the apparently true friend of Wallenstein, OCTAVIO PICCOLOMINI, to whom the commander is most warmly attached, without suspecting that he is sent to watch him and to lead him to ruin. Between the two stands Octavio's son MAX, a noble, straightforward youth, who admires the commander and honors him as a father, and at the same time is deeply in love with Wallenstein's daughter THEKLA. Thus is prepared the moral conflict in his soul, in which he soon has to choose between filial duty and love. To him the treachery of the great man seems inconceivable; and when his father warns him that SESIN, who has been conducting negotiations with the Swedes for Wallenstein, has been arrested, he will believe nothing of the whole affair, but will go to the duke and ask him himself.

WALLENSTEIN'S TOD (Death). The storm gathers in an ever more threatening aspect over the general, who now steps entirely into the foreground. He had played with dangerous thoughts, and is now driven to the fulfillment of them by the fact that his enemies have damaging evidence against him. WRANGEL, the Swedish general, convinces him that he can not retreat. Thus he comes to open revolt; he forms an alliance with the Swedes, and thereby completes his treachery, and seals his own doom. With obstinate blindness, he intrusts to Octavio Piccolomini the most important position, which the faithless friend (declared general-in-chief of the army by the secret command of the emperor) uses to win over to his side the generals, especially BUTLER, who had been the faithful devotee of Wallenstein. Under his influence whole regiments leave the duke, and once more swear allegiance to the emperor. Wallenstein, with a small remnant of his army, is proscribed, but even now he does not lose courage. The hardest trial for him is the desertion of Max Piccolomini. The catastrophe approaches with increasing suspense. Max seeks and finds a soldier's death in the tumult of battle; Thekla hastens to his grave, there to die. Her father's fate is sealed, and he withdraws to Eger, where he is soon assassinated.

With this piece Schiller became the favorite poet of the nation, and although it is open to criticism, it is nevertheless the greatest of German tragedies, and superior to the author's later works.

The technical mastery that he had gained in writing *Wallenstein,* and the joy he felt at its warm reception led the poet to devote all his powers to the drama. Before beginning a new production, however, he indulged a long-cherished desire by moving to Weimar. Here he resumed energetic work on MARIA STUART (1800).

The historical Mary Schiller presents the last part of Mary's life, and that we may better understand this portion, it will be well to look at her earlier years. MARY STUART, the daughter of James V, of Scotland, and Mary, of Lorraine, received her education at a cloister in France, and at the age

of fifteen was married to the Dauphin. Soon after her husband
came to the throne, both he and her mother died, and the young
queen returned to assume control of the Scottish government.
She still held claims to the throne of England, and on this account ELIZABETH denied her the privilege of passing through
England. Thus began the quarrel which became fatal to Mary.
On her arrival she passed from wantonness to crime. First she
married her relative DARNLEY, and then negotiated with the
Catholic power to such an extent as to turn all the Scottish lords
from her. When Darnley caused RIZZIO to be murdered at her
side, she desired to be freed from such a husband. The Earl of
BOTHWELL satisfied this wish by blowing up the house in which
the man was staying. The queen then married the murderer,
but the Scottish lords were so wrought up that they caused her
to be imprisoned, and then made her abdicate in favor of her
son. She escaped, and made her way to England, where she
hoped to influence Elizabeth to help her against her enemies.
She was disappointed, and was kept as a prisoner, first at one
castle and then at another, until she was finally brought to
Fotheringay in 1587.

Schiller's Mary Stuart
At this point *Maria Stuart* begins, and the rest of
the story is told according to Schiller. Here in
harsh imprisonment, the unhappy queen suffers for
the guilt of her earlier years. She is tried and condemned to
death, but her bitter enemy, ELIZABETH, can not make up her
mind to sanction the execution of the decree, although BURLEIGH,
her counselor, urges it. She hints to MORTIMER, the nephew of
Mary's keeper, that she would prefer to have the imprisoned
queen disposed of secretly. But she is mistaken in her tool.
While in France, Mortimer has gone over to the Catholic Church,
and is filled with the desire to set at liberty the queen whom he
admires and loves. Merely to gain time he pretends to go about
the murder. Count LEICESTER also loves Mary, and would gladly
rescue her, but he is afraid of such violent means as Mortimer
plans. He therefore contrives a meeting between the two queens,
by means of which—instead of the hoped-for reconciliation—a
complete rupture is brought about. MARY, led on by Elizabeth's
harsh and cutting behavior, gives vent to passionate language.
Elizabeth, whose pride is mortally wounded, can no longer think

of mercy. Leicester, who, to protect himself, has caused the arrest and death of Mortimer, succeeds in freeing himself from all suspicion in the mind of Elizabeth, and finally votes for Mary's death. Elizabeth signs the decree, which Burleigh at once executes.

General estimate In this tragedy Schiller has allowed himself free treatment of history; names, situations, and circumstances have been taken from history; but the tragic element has been created with true poetic fancy, and is made to appear as it might have been. The two queens have been painted by the artist according to the sympathy which he felt for the one, and the antipathy for the other, now in colors too bright, now too dark. Even the crisis, the meeting of the queens, is unhistorical, but dramatically it is of the utmost importance. The drama was first brought out in Weimar, and the author was so well satisfied with the reception that he said, "I am finally becoming master of the dramatic art." Yet this play is much inferior to *Wallenstein,* and by many is regarded as his weakest tragedy.

In the JUNGFRAU VON ORLEANS (Maid of Orleans, 1801) history and free invention are woven together; but the chief attraction lies in the magic spell of the romantic and religious inspiration of the heroine, her intercourse with the spirit world, her visions, and her national mission.

Historical Joan At the time represented, England and France had long been at war, and England had been so victorious that when Henry VI came to the throne, he was proclaimed king in a large part of northern France. The English pushed south, crossed the Loire, and were besieging Orleans, when there appeared the phenomenon of JOAN OF ARC. While watching her parents' flocks at their home in the village of Dom Remy, the Virgin Mary repeatedly appeared to her, urged her to free her country from the foreign rule, and equipped her with remarkable power. Obeying the command, she takes a vow of chastity, renounces all earthly happiness, rejects the wooing of her lover, RAIMOND, and bids her home and her people farewell.

She gains the confidence of the court of the Dauphin at Chinon, and clad in armor she leads the army against the enemy, kills every living creature that the god of battle sends against her, drives the enemy into flight, and leads the Dauphin to his coronation at Reims. According to history, this was the end of her course of heroism. In an attack which she made with a small army against the enemy, she was taken by the Burgundians, and turned over to the English, who burned her as a witch in 1431.

Schiller's Joan
To such a disgraceful end the poet could not allow his heroine to come; therefore, he allowed her saintly mission to prove also her doom. She suddenly plunges from her supernatural height, because in the hour of temptation she proves herself to be a weak woman who breaks her vow. She has rejected two suitors, DUNOIS and LA HIRE, without mercy she had stricken the enemy, and she has even resisted the ghost-like black knight; but finally the handsome young Englishman, LIONEL, fires her heart with human love; she conquers but can not kill him, now her power is gone. Under the consciousness of guilt, her spirit is broken. When her father, in the midst of the people, asks her if she "belongs to the pure and holy ones," she answers nothing, and remains silent while he heaps the heaviest of accusations upon her, for she believes it all comes from God. Rejected, banished, and proscribed as a witch, she wanders around in the mountains until the English find her. Once more she gains control of herself, and when Lionel wishes to protect her, and renews his proffer of love, she firmly rejects him. After this her old power returns; when she hears that the English are conquering, she breaks her bonds, rushes out into the tumult of battle, and dies as a victor.

Translations
At the request of the duke, Goethe had translated for the Weimar theater two pieces from Voltaire, *Mahomet* and *Tancred*. Schiller, who always was interested in his friend's plans, joined with him in an effort to prepare several foreign dramas for the German stage. He translated Shakespeare's *Macbeth,* and *Turandot* from the Italian poet Gozzi.

Schiller ennobled

Although a great favorite of the duke and duchess, Schiller had no *von* before his name, and was not eligible to move in the court society. His wife possessed this right by birth, but lost it by marrying a man who did not belong to the nobility. This was frequently a matter of inconvenience, and the duke, wishing to show his appreciation, petitioned the emperor for Schiller's elevation to the rank of nobility. The patent was handed to the poet in the fall of 1802, and although he valued the honor very little for himself, he did appreciate it for the sake of his wife and children.

A whole year passed before Schiller went to work on another original drama, and he was for some time uncertain as to what subject he would select. During a summer's convalescence he read Greek poetry, and was influenced by his reading toward a plan which he had long had in mind. He was perfectly satisfied that his special strength was in dramatizing historical events, and he therefore always preferred to use some existing story rather than create a new one. The *Œdipus Tyrannus* of Sophocles, had appealed to him, and he had sought long for some subject offering advantages equal to this. As he found none, he invented DIE BRAUT VON MESSINA (Bride of Messina, 1803), modeling it close after Sophocles's play. This time the poet made a bold experiment, writing the play in rhyme, and introducing a chorus, in imitation of the classical drama. All his rhythmical genius, and the richest of his rhetoric, were devoted to the task; but the result was, and still is, doubtful. It is occasionally played, but it can not be called a favorite with the public.

The PRINCE OF MESSINA has seen in a dream two laurel trees, and between them a lily, which turns into flame and destroys everything around it. An astrologer interprets this to mean that his wife is to bear a daughter who will destroy his two sons and his whole family. When the daughter is born, he at once commands her to be thrown into the sea. ISABELLA, his

wife, had dreamed that she saw a child playing in the grass, and
at its feet lay quietly a lion and an eagle. A monk explains this
to mean that she is to become the mother of—

> "A daughter, sent
> To knit the warring spirits of her sons
> In bonds of tender love."

Trusting to the happy dream and its interpretation, she rescues
BEATRICE, the daughter of blessing, and provides for her education in a convent. Years pass by, the prince dies without knowing of the existence of his daughter, and his two sons, MANUAL
and CÆSAR, always quarreling, but held in check by their father,
break out into passionate strife at his grave, and threaten to drag
the whole state into civil war. Finally, however, the mother
succeeds in bringing them to terms of peace, and then discloses
to them the secret of their sister at the convent. Each of them
in turn acknowledges that he is in love, and promises to bring
his loved one to her on that very day. Great is Isabella's
rejoicing.

With terrible rapidity the change comes. DIEGO, the old
servant who has been sent after Beatrice, returns, and announces
that she has been carried off by pirates. Soon it appears that
both brothers love the same maiden, whom Manuel has often
visited as his loved one, and whom Cæsar has only seen. As the
latter finds her in his brother's arms, he believes that he has
been deceived, and at once stabs his brother. Too late comes the
discovery that the maiden is their sister. Paying no attention to
the entreaties of his sister and his mother, he kills himself at his
brother's bier. Thus the curse and the two oracles are fulfilled;
the princely house is desolate.

WILHELM TELL followed in 1804, and met with unprece-
dented approval in Weimar and Berlin. This, his last and by
many critics regarded as his best drama, illustrates the
beautiful way in which the two poets aided each other. The
subject and much of the material he received from Goethe,
who, while traveling in Switzerland, formed the plan of writing an epic with Tell as the hero. He studied the scenery,
got together the historical data, and kept the matter in mind

for two or three years. Finally deciding that the subject was better fitted for dramatic treatment, he turned his material over to Schiller, keeping only a description of a sunrise among the Alps, which he used in the opening scene of the second part of *Faust*. Schiller's intense imagination soon assimilated the foreign material, and he has worked the subject, scenery, and sentiment into beautiful harmony. From beginning to end the reader or hearer finds himself carried into the mountain homes of a brave and oppressed people, with all the beauties of their valleys around them.

When Albrecht of Austria became emperor of Germany (1298), he endeavored to bring under Austrian rule the Swiss Cantons, Schwyz, Uri, and Unterwalden, which had long been subject to the German emperor only. To further his purpose, Albrecht sent two governors, GESSLER and LANDENBERG, who maltreated and oppressed the people in a tyrannical manner.

Many a messenger was sent to the imperial court to complain of the oppression, and they were all given to understand that their trials would cease as soon as they would subject themselves to the rule of Austria. Then a few of the leading men of the three cantons, WALTER FÜRST, WERNER STAUFFACHER, and ARNOLD VON MELCHTAL, enlist thirty others in their country's cause, and all meet at the Rütli, there to renew their old bond of independence, in order to shake off the foreign yoke.

From the nobility, the old BARON VON ATTINGHAUSEN is the only one on the side of the people, and on his deathbed he is rejoiced to hear what the people have decided to do, and that his nephew, ULRICH VON RUDENZ, has been won back to his people by the influence of his loved one, BERTHA VON BRUNECK.

In the meantime a man who was not at the Rütli because he was "not born to ponder and select," has freed the land from its most dangerous enemy, Gessler. This man was TELL. When commanded to bow before the ducal hat on the pole in Altorf, he refused to do so. To save his life he was compelled at Gessler's command to shoot an apple from his son's head. After a long struggle with himself, he performs the deed. Yet, because he had put a second arrow in his belt, which was intended for Gessler if the first one had injured his boy, he was bound and

taken to the boat which was to carry him to the dungeon at
Küssnacht. While on the way the boat gets into great danger;
Tell's bands are loosened that he may steer the craft through the
terrific storm; he sees a rocky projection near the water; guides
the boat close up to it, and leaps ashore.

Gessler reaches the land in safety, but as he is riding over
a narrow road to Küssnacht, Tell sends an arrow through his
heart. When the people hear of Tell's arrest, they decide not
to await until the apointed time for the uprising, but set about
the work at once. They rise in force all over the cantons, overthrow the strongholds, drive away the remaining governor, Landenberg, and make the land really free. Then comes the news
that the emperor has been murdered by his nephew. When
the murderer appears at Tell's house, alluding to the assassina-
tion of Gessler as a reason why he should receive hospitality, he
is told that there is no similarity between his deed and Tell's.

Yet Tell finally takes pity on the unhappy man, shows him
the way to Rome, where he is to confess all to the pope, and dismisses him well laden with necessaries for the trip. He is
scarcely gone, when the confederates come to greet the liberator
of the land, and to thank him for his service.

Estimate Except in the love episode between Rudenz and
Bertha, Schiller has followed closely the legend
as it was handed down by the chronicles. But under the
light of modern history this report proves to be largely
mythical; especially that part referring to Tell, which probably came from a very ancient myth well known in Denmark, Norway, and Iceland. Notwithstanding this, Schiller's
Tell is a person clear and distinct, destined to stand through
all time. We may apply to him the words the poet utters
in one of his lyrics: "That which has never and nowhere
happened, never grows old." In this play we see the same
tones that appear in his early dramas. Rousseau's glorification of nature and the primitive condition of the race; but
how much grander and purer is this idea here! In the first
of his dramas it was a tirade against the existing order of
things, here it is the overthrow of an unnatural element that

comes from without, and the rising of a glorious people and a glorious country to their natural rights. In the earlier dramas the author was iconoclastic, here in the maturity of his intellect, he is quite the opposite; he leads onward to what should be.

Wilhelm Tell was received with more enthusiasm than any of Schiller's other works. Written two years before the battle of Jena, it became familiar at a time when Germany was passing through the darkest period of her history; and the light of this drama seemed to shine into this darkness, and give her a hope of better days. As the years went by,

Political influence of Tell
it became more and more a bond between the representatives of German liberty. Its influence in uniting the numerous states against Napoleon was of importance, and then again in the war of 1870 the fundamental idea of the drama found a warm reception in the hearts of the people, and had much to do in leading them to the strong union now embodied in the German Empire.

Visit to Berlin
In the spring of 1804 he went to Berlin, where in honor of his visit all his dramas were acted, and as the poet took his place in the audience on the night when the *Braut* was to be played, the people greeted him with shouts and acclamations of joy. An effort was made to bring him to Berlin, but old associations and especially his relations with Goethe, kept him at the little "Athens of Germany." For the festivities attending the arrival of the young bride of the Crown Prince he wrote *Huldigung der Künste* (Homage of the Arts). Several plans for great dramas were under consideration, but only one, *Demetrius,* based on an episode from Russian history, had made any progress, when, while at work on the second act, death on May 9, 1805, ended the struggle which had been going on so long between that noble spirit and the shattered body that contained it.

His life was short, but in the span of a little more than forty-five years, he had experienced what few men with long lives have known; he had enjoyed the pleasure of tender and sympathetic love and friendship; and when at the sum-

General character-istics
mit of his fame, he had the satisfaction of knowing that, through his own energy, in spite of discouraging circumstances, he had gained a high place in the world, and had earned the love and gratitude of the German nation and the world at large.

From the standpoint of literary criticism or in reference to his influence on succeeding literature and thought in general, Schiller must be ranked below the great names, Homer, Dante, Shakespeare, and Goethe; he is to be classified rather with Vergil, Tasso, Corneille, Spenser, Byron, and Tennyson. However, to the great masses of the German people.

A national poet
he is the first and greatest poet, the one with whom the youth of Germany early become acquainted, and for whom the older people never lose their admiration. This veneration is due to his life as well as to his poetry, for he was a man of noble, pure, unselfish character, incapable of falsity, full of high ideals, a man who devoted the whole of his power to the service of the good, the true, and the beautiful. His rhythm and rhetoric have never been surpassed, and his poetry by its wide circulation and its natural genuineness has nourished in the German people the most noble sentiments—love for the fatherland, for freedom, for honor, for justice and truth, for friendship and fidelity.

Goethe's Old Age (1805-1832)

His loneliness
Goethe was much affected by the death of Schiller, and expressed his grief in the words: "I lose a friend, and in him, half of my existence." His loneliness became deeper on account of the sad events of the next few years. The battle of Jena in 1806 brought

to Weimar humiliation and suffering; the Duchess Amalia died in 1807, and in the following year the poet's mother. In 1808 he had an interview with Napoleon, and each was filled with admiration for the genius of the other. His time was now given largely to scientific work, yet he was always active with literary plans. In 1808 the first part of *Faust* appeared, and in the following year, his WAHLVERWANDT-SCHAFTEN (Elective Affinities).

The title of this novel is borrowed from the language of chemistry. The molecules of certain materials are irresistibly attracted to each other, and are always endeavoring to become united; they are said to have "affinity" for each other; the molecules of certain other materials are always repulsing each other; so in the human world certain persons are drawn to each other, while others are repelled, without the action of will power.

EDWARD and CHARLOTTE, who, as young people, have loved each other, but have been separated by circumstances, and led into uncongenial marriages, as widower and widow in later years have attained to the realization of their youthful dreams. They live in apparently happy married life, although what binds them is rather a friendly, mutual good will, than a deep, overpowering love. As soon as other persons who naturally have an "affinity" for them, come into their presence, the deception becomes apparent. The repelling and the attractive elements exert their influences as soon as Edward's friend, the CAPTAIN, and Charlotte's foster-daughter, OTTILIE, come into their circle. Charlotte is attracted to the Captain, and Edward to Ottilie. While the older pair strive against it, and the Captain leaves the house of his friends, Edward yields to temptation, and awakens in Ottilie the hope that, by an amicable separation from Charlotte, her lover may still be united with her. Edward's and Charlotte's child is drowned through the carelessness of Ottilie. In the presence of the corpse Charlotte makes up her mind to consent to the separation which she had heretofore refused to sanction. But the deplorable event has produced just the opposite effect upon the mind of Ottilie; she has recognized her wrong, and declares that she will never become Edward's wife. And although Edward continues to urge her, she remains firm in her determination, but seeks death by abstaining from food and drink. Edward, overcome by grief, soon follows her to the grave.

Estimate The novel met with boundless admiration on the one side, yet on the other, with sharpest criticism. Many regarded it as the highest type of the modern novel; others called it stilted in style, senile in thought, and some even went so far as to call it immoral. In a general way we may say that the subject of the novel is marriage, which is here more seriously considered than in any of Goethe's other works.

DICHTUNG UND WAHRHEIT (Poetry and Truth, 1811-17), his autobiography, shows in a classical form the experiences and struggles of his life up to the time he went to Weimar. His object was to represent the principles that had been of influence in his life. Yet from the very title itself, and from what has been learned of him since it was written, it is clearly no true historical record. Many events are changed to suit his fancy and to fit into his artistic plan; many circumstances and even persons are far from being in exact accordance with the truth. As a whole, however, it does form a very fine and truthful picture of the man and the times in which he lived.

While the poet was telling the story of his early life, he also composed many poems, among them *Johanna Sebus, Der Totentanz* (The Dance of Death), and *Die Wandelnde Glocke* (The Walking Bell). A hard blow came to him in 1816, in the death of his "little wife," who had lived with him for thirty years, and whom he loved more dearly than the world generally believed. His only son was married the following year, and thus new life was brought into his home. This son died in Rome in 1830, but his wife and her three children cheered the poet's last days with loving attention.

Goethe and the Napoleonic oppression

When all Germany was struggling to throw off the hated yoke of Napoleon, Goethe turned a cold heart toward his country's cause, and sought distraction in the study of the poetry of the East. He was led to this through a translation of the Persian poet HAFIS. The result of this study is the *Westöstlicher Divan* (West-Eastern Divan, 1815-19), a series of poems in Eastern dress but German in form and content, in which he wished to bring the East and West together. In them Goethe is represented under the name of "Hatem;" and the "Suleika" of the poems was his friend Marianne von Willemer, who in reality wrote several of the poems in the collection.

Fiftieth Anniversary

On Nov. 7, 1825, a celebration was held in honor of the fiftieth year of his service in Weimar. On this occasion the duke assured the friend of his youth that "he regarded the coming of Goethe to his court, there to remain during his life, as one of the greatest honors of his reign." Karl August died in 1828; the duchess and Goethe's only son died two years later.

In 1829 WILHELM MEISTERS WANDERJAHRE (Travels) was completed. This novel was intended to carry out the ideas contained in the *Lehrjahre,* and "to show the influence of a many-sided life on the development of a gifted man." The work lacks unity. It is largely a series of short romances, and among them all are woven Goethe's ideas about state, society, family, education, and numerous other things.

FAUST, the greatest and grandest of his works, was completed in the poet's eighty-third year, and may be called his life work. Even in his home at Frankfort, the boy, as he was studying alchemy, had given serious thought to this subject. Even there he became acquainted with the folksbook of Dr. Faust, and later saw the same theme represented in a puppet show. The year 1772 he designates as the birth-

Suggestion of the drama

year of his drama, which at that time rose up before him in its general features. He had just finished his studies at Strassburg, from that time on the plan of the production was ever before him, and he wrote the various scenes as they individually attracted him. His chief activity on the first part, however, falls in the years 1773-75; some other portions were composed in the eighties, the witches' kitchen scene while in Rome. In 1790 that part which was finished appeared as *Ein Fragment.*

At Schiller's solicitation, he resumed his work after a long pause, but not until three years after his friend's death did the first part appear under the title of *Faust, eine Tragödie.* Although the poet regarded the first part as merely a fragment, sixteen years passed before he resumed work on the second part, which was completed seven years later, in 1831. He sealed it, and commanded that it should not be published until after his death. Thus the poem compasses the whole life of its author; from boyhood to the gray-haired old man. However much personal experiences may be there portrayed, they are at the same time the experiences common to every thoughtful, investigating, struggling man. It may well be called the drama of modern times.

Prefixed to the drama is a "Dedication," written in 1797, when the middle-aged man resumed work on the drama that had for some time remained untouched. In it he expresses the feelings that come to him as he takes up the work which he had begun when on the verge of manhood. He recalls friends and experiences of twenty-five years before, and contrasts them with his surroundings of that time

The prologues

Two prologues serve as an introduction. The first, the Prelude on the Stage, brings out the contrast between the standpoint of the theater director and that of the poet; the former wishes to please the crowd, while the latter wishes to produce something genuinely artistic, something that will last for all time. The second, the Prologue in

Heaven, is partially modeled on the book of Job. Accompanying three archangels, who come to worship the Lord, is MEPHIS-
TOPHELES, the wicked, fallen spirit, who ridicules man, "the little
god of the world," and especially DR. FAUST, whom the Lord
acknowledges as his servant. He goes even further, and impu-
dently says to the Lord:—

> "There's still a chance to gain him,
> If unto me full leave you give,
> Gently on *my* road to train him."

The Lord, expressing his confidence in Faust, grants the
privilege.

**First
Part**
In the first part of the tragedy, Faust appears, in
his study, lamenting that all his studies have given
him no satisfaction—for this reason he turns to
magic. Full of the desire to learn something more than is
allotted to common mortals, he conjures the spirits. The EARTH
SPIRIT appears in a form which he can scarcely endure and then
tells him that he is like the spirit he can comprehend.

Driven to despair by this repulse, and annoyed by his assistant, WAGNER, he decides to take poison.

He has already put the cup to his lips, when he hears from
the neighboring church the chorus of angels singing the Easter
song, "Christ is arisen!" Although he has no faith in a divine
message, these sounds remind him of his childhood, and check
him in his mad deed.

Accompanied by his assistant, he takes a long walk in the
country, and in the evening he feels a longing for revelation as it
appears in the New Testament. He takes down the original text,
begins to translate it into German, and while thus occupied, he
is interrupted by the howling and growling of a dog that had fol-

**Mephis-
topheles**
lowed him from the fields. He soon sees that the
animal's nature is something else, and at once begins
to try the effect of magic upon him. Under this
treatment the dog soon swells up into a cloud of smoke from
which steps Mephistopheles, whose real character proves to be
thoroughly Satanic.

He offers his services to Faust in this world, if, in the world
to come, he may have Faust's soul. Faust in his disgust at the
world accepts with the following words:—

"When thus I hail the moment flying:
  '*Ah,* *still* *delay—thou art so fair!*'
Then bind me in thy bonds undying,
  My final ruin then declare!"

The problem is for Mephistopheles to make Faust so happy that he will wish for nothing more, although he knows that it will cost him his soul. But how can happiness be evolved from evil? Mephistopheles now leads his companion out into the world to see, if in some place or other and in some way or other,

Auerbach's Cellar he can not entice him into saying that he is perfectly happy. They first go to a wild drinking-frolic in Auerbach's Cellar. Instead of being pleased with the wild reveling there, Faust is disgusted. Mephistopheles, realizing that Faust is too old to be tempted by the things that tempt most men, decides that he must have his youth restored,

Witch's kitchen takes him to a witch's kitchen, and has the witch give him a drink which will bring back his youth. Next come the simple, exquisite scenes of the MAR-GARET episode. Faust first sees her as she comes from the church, and is repulsed when he offers himself as escort. Through the assistance of his fiendish companion and "neighbor MARTHA,"

Martha's garden an interview is brought about in Martha's garden, in which there is a mutual declaration of love. The better part of his nature urges him to leave the innocent girl, for fear he may do her harm; but Mephistopheles, by recalling her beauty, and by painting her loneliness and her longing for her lover, brings him back to her again. Margaret asks

Margaret Scenes him about his religion, and in his answers we find Faust's confession of faith. At this point the tragic part of the story begins.

Margaret unintentionally poisons her mother, and is herself ruined; yet we feel that she is a helpless victim, and that the original purity of her nature can not be stained. When she realizes the extent of her crime and disgrace, she goes to the Virgin, and offers a prayer, a passionate appeal of a loving and suffering heart.

But the image can do her no good. Another crime is added. Faust is attacked by Margaret's brother, and the brother is slain. Faust and Mephistopheles flee from the city, and she is left alone. She goes to the cathedral, but the organ tones are like

the judge's trumpet, and the evil spirit drives the sting of a guilty conscience still deeper into her heart. Faust's conscience keeps pricking him, and he is unhappy, too. To deaden his con-
Brocken science, Mephistopheles takes him to the wild, weird, diabolical atmosphere of the Brocken on Walpurgis-Night. All the revelries of the witches have no attraction for Faust, whose mind and heart are with Margaret. Now comes the information that Margaret has killed her child, and that on
Margaret in prison the verge of insanity, she lies in prison, awaiting death at the hand of the executioner. Faust is beside himself; wildly he rages against Mephistopheles for having concealed from him these facts, and demands from him her rescue. Magic black horses carry them to the prison. Faust hastens in to free his loved one, but she knows him not, she understands him not. When she finally recognizes "the friend's voice," she can not make up her mind to follow him, and when the repulsive form of Mephistopheles appears, she quickly gives herself up to the judgment of God, rather than to seek protection in such company. "Thine am I, Father! rescue me!" she prays, and is heard; for in answer to Mephistopheles's scornful words: "She is judged," there comes from above the voice of mercy: "She is saved." Faust is drawn away by his companion, and as he departs, he hears the pleading, warning words, "Henry! Henry!"

This is all that most people know of *Faust*. But the evolution of the great plan is merely begun. Of all the experiences common to men, Faust has been drawn merely to love, and this has been so tormented by conscience and remorse, that the moment of perfect happiness has not yet come to him. The compact with Mephistopheles still continues, he has not yet won his wager—has not yet led Faust to say, "Ah, still delay—thou art so fair." When the two started to see the world, they were to see first the "little world," and then the "greater world." The former, meaning the experiences, the emotions, and passions of individuals, we have portrayed in the first part; the latter meaning the experiences of life in a broader field of activity, among men, and in stations where one's influence is felt by thousands or by a whole race, we have represented in the second part.

Second Part

The second part is crowded with characters, and the events are represented on so large a scale that the element of allegory had to be introduced, and single persons made to typify whole classes of society. He passes from the experiences through which he touches all men, and rises to those which touch merely people who think and aspire. Some considerable time is supposed to have passed between the events of the first and second parts. In the opening scenes we have embodied a very important feature of Goethe's creed. He believed that a moral wound could be healed, and that the influences of time and nature were the very best means of healing such wounds. He believed, too, that the very best atonement for a wrong committed, was not to be made by brooding over the recollection of it, but in being restored to cheerfulness and courage and hope.

FAUST appears sleeping on the shore of a beautiful Alpine lake, surrounded by elves who are to represent symbolically the influences of time and nature in causing him to recover from his grief at the downfall of Margaret. He awakens to an entrancing scene of a sunrise among the Alps—a scene which Goethe kept when he bequeathed his material to Schiller for the *William Tell* (153). He is calmed and refreshed, he has forgotten the past, and is ready to face the activities of life once more. In fact, he is so thoroughly relieved from his consciousness of grief and crime, that with one exception he never refers to the first part. With the help of MEPHISTOPHELES he starts out in new ways to be helpful to people wherever he can. They first appear at the court of the EMPEROR, whom they help from financial embarrassment by the invention of paper money. They remain there amusing the emperor with all sorts of tricks, and finally he desires a special exhibition of Faust's art; he commands him to produce at his court the shades of PARIS and HELEN. With the aid of Mephistopheles, Faust succeeds in doing this, and while the court are occupied in their various remarks about their beauty, Faust himself is seized by a passionate adoration of Helen, and he is on the point of grasping her, when the spirit disappears. Faust falls to the floor, Mephistopheles picks him up, and carries him to his old laboratory.

In the second act he is represented as lying there, and while he is asleep, his former assistant, WAGNER, has produced a human form by putting together the various elements that are found in the body; but he is unable to put life into this form, until Mephistopheles helps him with superhuman power. This creation, called HOMUNCULUS, advises that Faust be carried to Greece, that he may recover from his passion for Helen. Mephistopheles and Homunculus carry Faust through the air to Greece.

Here is introduced a Grecian Walpurgis-Night in contrast to the Gothic one in the first part. Faust is occupied with only one thought—to find Helen, but his search is in vain. Finally he goes to Hades to seek her there, but of this errand we hear nothing more.

In the third act, generally called "The Helena," Helen is represented as fleeing from her husband, and coming for protection to a Gothic castle, the owner of which is Faust. They are married, and a son, EUPHORION, is born to them. Helen is not only the ideal of the beautiful, but also the classical element in literature and art, while Faust represents the romantic element. Euphorion is therefore the union of these two elements. He is the perfect embodiment of Goethe's own poetry; but just at the time he was writing this act, the English poet Byron died, and his death affected Goethe so much that he decided to make Euphorion a distinct representative of Byron. At the close of the act, Euphorion dies, and Helen disappears, leaving only her garments, which turn into clouds and bear Faust away.

In the fourth act, Faust has been carried back home, and now turns from the service of the beautiful to the service of the state, or, as it might better be stated, to the service of the people. He longs for activity, and soon begins to recover from the sea a large tract of land by building a dike and by draining, thus making a home for large numbers of colonists. Then he helps the emperor suppress a rebellion, and in return for this service he is given the title to a large tract of marshy ground on the seashore.

In the fifth act, the aged Faust lives in a palace, and rules over a large and thickly populated territory, that he has reclaimed from the sea. Where formerly waves were rolling, there are now to be seen meadow and garden, village and forest. He is, however, not entirely satisfied; Mephistopheles has mixed evil with the good. In a midnight scene before the palace, four gray women approach: they are Want, Necessity, Guilt, and Care. The first three retire, but Care slips in through the keyhole. Faust bids her defiance, but she breathes on his eyes and blinds him. His power is not broken, saying that one mind is enough for a thousand hands, he urges his men on to the work of draining the last swamp in the whole tract. He hears the work going on, and in his mind sees the happy moment when the whole will be finished, and millions living there. This thought fills him with joy, and he cries:—

> "Then dared I hail the moment fleeing,
> 'Ah, *still delay—thou art so fair!*'"

These are his last words, and with them he drops dead. Mephistopheles, counting on the contract, summons his angels of darkness to carry the soul of Faust away; but as they aproach, a light falls from above, and a chorus of angels come strewing roses and chanting. While Mephistopheles and his messengers stop to gaze at the beautiful sight, these angels carry the immortal part of Faust upward, singing as they rise:—

> "The noble spirit now is free,
>   And saved from evil scheming;
> Whoe'er aspires unweariedly
>   Is not beyond redeeming.
> And if he feels the grace of love
>   That from on high is given,
> The blessed hosts, that wait above,
>   Shall welcome him to heaven!"

These words give us the elements of Faust's salvation, and we see that they are harmonious with the Lord's statement in the *Prologue in Heaven:*—

> "Then stand abashed, when thou art forced to say:
>   A good man, through obscurest aspiration,
>   Has still an instinct of the one true way."

In summing up the beauties of the poem, Bayard Taylor says:

"There is nothing in the literature of any country with which we can fairly compare it. There is no other poem, which, like this, is the work of a whole life, and which deals with the profoundest problems of all life. It is so universally comprehensive that every reader finds in it reflections of his faith and philosophy. The poem embodies all the finest qualities of Goethe's mind,—his rich, ever-changing rhythm, his mastery over the elements of passion, his simple realism, his keen irony, his serene wisdom, and his most sacred aspiration. The more it is studied, the wider and farther it spreads its intellectual horizon until it grows to be so far and dim that the physical and spiritual spheres are blended together."

Completion of life work When *Faust* was finished, Goethe regarded his work in the world as over, and whatever of life was given him afterward, he called a gift. Only a few months were granted him; he died over fourscore years of age, on March 22, 1832, and was buried beside his friend Schiller in the grand ducal vault in Weimar.

Place in literature He stands in German literature as the first and by far the greatest figure, and also one of the greatest in the literature of the world. His genius was universal, enabling him to work with ease and success in all kinds of literature; he unites more than any other person in perfect harmony, nature and art, life and poetry, form and content. In him the Classical period reached its height, and if we compare him with the other men of this period, we will see that in him were united Klopstock's ability to enrich the language, Lessing's clearness of vision and bold individuality, Wieland's elegance and grace, Herder's universality, and Schiller's rhythm and rhetoric. His works and his influence will endure as long as language lasts.

JEAN PAUL FRIEDRICH RICHTER, better known under the name of Jean Paul (1763-1825), was reared under circumstances of privation, and after the death of his father, who was a country preacher and school-teacher, the family were left in abject poverty. He entered the University of Leipzig as a student of theology, making his living by tutoring or any other work that came in his way. Here he read an incredible number of books of various kinds, and from this random reading he collected a whole library of extracts, which he afterward used in his novels. His finances became more and more strained and forced him to writing. Some of his attempts were successful, but several hard years he had to spend in privation, part of the time at home with his mother, and part of the time teaching. In 1790 he struck his own field, the idyl, and *Das Leben des vergnügten Schulmeisterleins Wuz* (Life of the Little Contented Schoolmaster, Wuz), which is one of the most attractive of his works, appeared and founded the reputation that increased with his succeeding humorous novels.

Die Unsichtbare Loge (The Invisible Lodge) made him at once popular, and opened the way for a life free from financial care.

CAPTAIN FALKENBERG has his son GUSTAV, to protect him from the temptations of life, brought up in a cave, under the care of a pious teacher, who prepares him for death and the future world. One day it is announced to the boy that he is dead, and thereupon he is brought to the light of the world, which now appears as heaven to him. His sensitive nature rejoices at the pleasures of the world; in a blind beggar-boy he finds a comrade, and in a noble maiden he finds a sweetheart. The court to which he comes proves to be his destruction, because there he becomes entangled in the net of a heartless coquette. Through the secret power of the Invisible Lodge he is saved and purified. Here the novel breaks off, and has remained, like so many of Richter's, incomplete.

In Weimar Soon after the appearance of this novel he spent some time in Weimar, winning the favor of all the ladies and of Herder and Wieland, but Goethe and Schiller could not become enthusiastic over him. His greatest

11

novels, which at the time of their publication aroused much enthusiasm, are now almost forgotten.

Hesperus depicts the love of VICTOR, Gustav of the *Invisible Lodge,* at a somewhat riper age, for KLOTILDE, a high-minded, sentimental girl, and how they overcome all obstacles to their union.

PRINCE ALBANO, the hero of *Titan,* in ignorance of his parentage, is brought up by simple upright people, that he may be protected from the enervating influences of court life. He passes through many trials and deceptions, before his love for PRINCESS IODINE awakens his better nature, and develops him into a wise and noble ruler.

Flegeljahre portrays in the two brothers WALT and VULT, the dreamy idealist, and the realist acquainted with the world, a part of the poet's own nature.

One of the best idyls is *Das Leben des Quintus Fixlein.* The hero is the fifth assistant teacher in a city school, he is promoted and finally becomes a parson and marries a poor and unattractive girl of the nobility.

Place in literature
Richter had a genuine gift of humor, a strong imagination, and a happy faculty of catching the poetical aspect of everything. His narrative is broad and animated, full of life and action, but his materials are seldom artistically joined together. He runs from one extreme of feeling to another, and incongruous subjects are jostled together in sentences lacking in elegance and grace. He abounds in metaphors, parentheses, and digressions. Although he did influence the humor of his time, and although his contemporaries honored him highly, and thought the twentieth century would rank him among the great men of literature, the closing nineteenth century esteems him less than ever, and his work has influenced literature less than that of numerous men of inferior talent.

CHAPTER X

THE ROMANTIC SCHOOL.

Rise of classical influence

Goethe's long life enabled him to witness many a change in the intellectual life of Germany. In his earlier days there was a love for the historical past of Germany, and imaginative writers delighted to people the forests with bards and druids, to dwell on the beauties of Gothic temples, and to sing of the knights of the Middle Ages. Toward the close of the century, however, all this tendency had vanished before the influence of classical antiquity, and Germany became flooded with classical fashion; the churches became ancient temples, all the arts strove after classical form, and the ladies imitated the dress and manners of the women of Greece. Germany's greatest poets, GOETHE and SCHILLER, both attained their highest development in poetic art while writing under the influence of classical study. During Goethe's advancing years, or at the transition from the eighteenth to the nineteenth centuries, there came a strong reactionary influence. Schiller's *Jungfrau von Orleans* and *Wilhelm Tell* mark a return to the themes of the Middle ages.

Reaction from classical influence

The tendencies that had been strong before the classic influence arose, again asserted themselves, and the admiration of classical antiquity became merely one among many other influences. To these new tendencies was given the name ROMANTICISM, and the poets who cultivated them were called ROMANTICISTS. The eighteenth century had been largely one of cold reason; everything had to be reduced to the level of common sense; the imaginative and the poetic had been almost banished. It was called the Age of Enlightenment, and against this the Romanticists strove. They combated the prevalent idea that poetry and life are a contradiction, and strove to realize the unity of the two. They wished to make poetry the aim and center of their lives. In contrast with the classic antiquity, the Romanticists chose as

Admiration for Middle Ages their great source of inspiration the Middle Ages of Germany, with their knights and their services of love; they were much more inclined to the Romish religion with its forms and symbols than to the rationalism that had become so prevalent; and in place of a dry, cold idea of life, they cherished one permeated with poetry and song. From mediæval Germany they turned to the Romance nations, then opened up the legendary world of the Orient. Their attention was also given to the fantastic myths of the North, and finally to the gigantic works of Shakespeare.

Just as their principles lacked definiteness and clearness, so the members of the Romantic School, although talented men, were not richly endowed with poetic creative power.

Contributions to literature They were strong in criticism and in scientific investigation. Although their poetic productions are not of great importance and have already been forgotten, their influence is strongly felt in all the lines of intellectual life. From the Romantic School arose the great German sciences of archeology, mythology, and philology; to the same source is due the new impulse in science of history; from these same tendencies there came new life into German painting; and music, too, received new ideas. One of the greatest services of this school, however, is the opening up of the poetry of all nations to the German people. DANTE and TASSO, CALDERON and CERVANTES, became known in Germany. SHAKESPEARE became a real German poet through the translation of A. W. Schlegel. Their activity was extended to Greece, Persia, and India, and from the study of these numerous languages, there arose the science of comparative philology.

The founders and the leaders of the Romantic School were the Schlegel brothers.

AUGUST WILHELM SCHLEGEL (1767-1845) was born in Hanover, studied in Göttingen, and taught some four years in Amsterdam. He then became connected with the University in Jena. Here he became acquainted with Goethe and Schiller, and contributed to their magazine, but soon broke with them and founded a review of his own, the *Athenäum,* which became the organ of the Romantic School. In 1801 he went to Berlin, and gave lectures on literature and art. After 1804 he traveled in company with Madame de Staël through Germany, Italy, Denmark, and Sweden. During the wars of 1813 and 1814 he was secretary to the crown prince of Sweden, and wrote most of his proclamations. In 1818 he was called to the University of Bonn as professor of literature. His own literary productions are marked by perfectness of form, but are lacking in real poetic value. As a translator he has done excellent service, and in however many respects some later translations of Shakespeare may be praiseworthy, his will always be a standard. And the same may be said of his translation of Calderon. His *Lectures on Dramatic Art and Literature* are noted for critical keenness and ability.

FRIEDRICH SCHLEGEL (1772-1829) was at first destined to a mercantile career, but at the age of sixteen he changed his plans and devoted himself to study. At Göttingen and Leipzig he became prominent for his linguistic powers and his thorough knowledge of Greek and Roman literature. Going to Jena he assisted his brother on the *Athenäum,* and soon accepted the ideas of Romanticism. One of the fundamental principles of this school—that poetry and life should not be separated, but that life should be permeated with poetry—he sought to expound in his morally and æsthetically offensive novel *Lucinde,* which glorifies unrestrained and unlawful love. His other poetical writings (the tragedy

Alarkos), with the exception of a few lyric poems, are of little importance. His service was in the line of translation, and in the science of philology and literature; his lectures on the *History of Ancient and Modern Literature* form the basis upon which the modern science of literary history rests.

LUDWIG TIECK (1773-1853) was born in Berlin, and received his university education for the most part at Göttingen, where he devoted his attention to the study of modern languages, especially English. Even at this time he arranged for the German stage an edition of Shakespeare's *Tempest*. He lived a short time in Jena and became acquainted with the other members of the Romantic School. During a visit to Rome, he studied the poetry of the Middle High German period, and published many minnesongs and other poems of the Middle Ages. For some years he led a wandering life, but finally settled in Dresden, where he began his writing of stories, and founded the art of public reading, in which he stands without out a peer. In 1841 he was called by the king to Berlin, where he remained until his death.

Public reader

He was not endowed with creative poetic genius, but by his rich talents he was able to comprehend the various times and spirits of literature, and to bring something new from them; and one of his first services was to bring the old myths and stories to new life. He prepared an excellent translation of Cervantes' *Don Quixote,* and has enjoyed renown for the translation of Shakespeare; but his part in this work consisted merely in the revision of the work of his daughter and of Count Baudissin. His songs and romances are for the most part forgotten. His comedies are dramatized fairy tales in which he criticizes the literary follies of the times. In two of his dramas, *Emperor Octavian* and *Genoveva,* he developed all the leading ideas of the Romantic School. He wrote also a large number of romances and *novellen*.[1] In the latter he was remarkably successful, and still stands among the very first writers of this kind of literature. In *Franz Sternbald's Wanderungen* (Franz Sternbald's Travels) he follows the plan of Goethe's *Wilhelm Meister*. The hero, a pupil of Albrecht Dürer, while in Italy, attains to the ideal in art, as that ideal is set forth in the Romantic School. The following are probably the best of his "novellen," *Dichterleben* (A Poet's Life), in which he portrays Shakespeare's youth; *Tod des Dichters* (A Poet's Death), in which he writes of the unhappy love of the Portuguese poet Camoens, and his tragic end; and the delightful little stories, *Die Gesellschaft auf dem Lande* (Society in the Country), *Musicalische Leiden und Freuden* (Musical Joys and Sorrows), and *Des Lebens Ueberfluss* (Life's Superabundance).

FRIEDRICH VON HARDENBERG (1772-1801), better known under the nom de plume of NOVALIS, was probably the most gifted poet of the younger Romanticists. He studied at Jena while Schiller was professor there, and later entered on a business career, but his life was saddened by the death of the young woman to whom he was engaged. Deeply afflicted by this, he wrote his *Hymnen an die Nacht* (Hymns to the Night), in which he gave expression to his morbid longing for death, and yet at the same time, the simple faith of his childhood. Soon a second engagement brought him happiness, and he once more turned to poetry. In 1799 he read to the Romanticists his *Geistliche Lieder* (Spiritual Songs), several of which have found a lasting place in the standard hymn-books. At the suggestion of Tieck, he began his novel, *Heinrich von Ofterdingen,* which, however, was only half done when he died.

---

[1]The German equivalent for our word "novel" is "Roman." The term "Novelle" was introduced by the Romantic School, and is applied to a short story, simple in its make-up, and whose essence is a study of character and situation.

CLEMENS BRENTANO (1788-1842), in connection with his brother-in-law, ACHIM VON ARNIM (1781-1831), published during the years 1806-08 *Des Knaben Wunderhorn* (The Boy's Wonderhorn), an excellent collection of folksongs. Of his own writings may be mentioned: *Geschichte vom braven Kasperl und der schonen Annerl* (Honest Kasper and Pretty Annie), a touching story; *Gockel, Hinkel, und Gackeleia,* a humorous fairy-tale; and the lyrics, *Die Gottesmauer* (The Churchyard Wall), *An eine Kranke* (To a Sick Woman), *Nach Sevilla* (To Saville), *Die lustigen Musikanten* (The Merry Minstrels), and *Die Lore Lay.* He produced his best work in the historical novel, *Die Kronenwächter* (Guards of the Crown), which contains some masterly pictures of the time of the Reformation.

FRIEDRICH BARON DE LA MOTTE FOUQUÉ (1777-1843), a descendant from a family of French emigrants, after several years in the army, retired to private life. Through the influence of A. W. Schlegel he turned his attention to literature and became widely read. His renown was due to the romances of chivalry that were devoured by the public during the first decade of this century. Two of his, worthy of mention, are *Der Zauberring* (The Magic Ring) and *Die Fahrten Thiodulfs des Isländers* (The Journeys of Thiodulf the Icelander). Although formless and fantastic, they represent the customs and life of the Middle Ages. They were very popular among various classes, but his succeeding novels were written in the same general manner, and the public became tired of them. His popularity was short lived; all that he had written was soon forgotten, except one fairy-tale, *Undine* (1811), which has kept his name in a favorable place.

UNDINE, the foster daughter of a fisherman and his wife, is a water-nymph, and as such had been born without a soul. According to legendary lore such creatures receive a soul as soon as they marry. The Knight HULDBRAND VON RINGSTETTEN falls in love with the cunning, smiling girl, and marries her. The wild, whimsical being becomes gentle and mild, and thoroughly devoted to the earnest man. But her uncle, the old KÜHLEBORN, tries to entice her back into her native element; furthermore, BERTALDA comes to the castle to disturb the peace of the young lovers. Although Huldbrand loves Undine, he feels himself drawn toward the human Bertalda. When, one day, old Kühleborn has robbed Bertalda of an ornament, Huldbrand chides Undine severely for having anything more to do with her former relatives. Thereupon she leaves him and returns to the waves. The knight now marries Bertalda, but on the wedding day Undine rises from the water and kills the knight with a kiss.

Only in the productions of two writers has the romantic drama lived on the stage. They are Kleist and Werner.

Romantic drama HEINRICH VON KLEIST (1777-1811) lived a short, wandering, morbid life, without finding any appreciation of his talent or his works. It remained for the succeeding generations to realize that this unfortunate man was the first great dramatic genius since Schiller, and to give to his dramas the immortality they deserve. He wrote several of real merit, of which the following are doubtless the best:

1. DIS KÄTCHEN VON HEILBRONN. This, a drama of chivalry, is truly romantic, and reminds the reader of Schiller's *Jungfrau von Orleans*. The heroine, KÄTCHEN, supposed to be the daughter of an armorer in Heilbronn, who has brought her up, is devotedly attached to Count WETTER VON STRAHL, whom she follows everywhere, although he drives her away from him with a whip as he would a dog. This devotion is due to animal magnetism and somnambulism. During one of her somnambulistic states she discloses the fact that she is in reality the daughter of the emperor, who acknowledges her and gives her to the count for his wife.

2. DER ZERBROCHENE KRUG (The Broken Pitcher) made an absolute failure in Weimar, but somewhat later became successful in Berlin, and has been a popular comedy since. It is one of the best comedies in the language. The author paints a strong picture

of a very amusing court scene, in which the judge in his vain efforts to convict a person on trial, proves himself to be the guilty man.

3. DIE HERMANNSSCHLACHT (Herman's Flight). In this the author gives vent to his anger at the disgrace of his country under the yoke of Napoleon, and shows his people how that yoke ought to be thrown off. He describes the struggle of the early Germans under Hermann against the invading Romans under Varus; but Varus and his army are merely a disguise for Napoleon and the French.

4. PRINCE FRIEDRICH VON HOMBURG. In this piece also somnambulism plays an important part. The prince, contrary to order, has attacked the enemy and won a victory. The Great Elector subjects him to trial before the court-marshal. In this trial it appears that the prince was in a somnambulistic state when the order was received, and, furthermore, in the same state had betrayed his love to the niece of the Great Elector. The conflict is solved in romantic fashion; the prince is acquitted, and he marries the niece. This is a patriotic production of the highest kind, but has never received the praise due to its merits.

Kleist wrote many lyric poems, and was a first-rate story-teller. The best of his "novellen" is *Michael Kohlhaas,* in which he tells the story of a horse-trader of the time of Luther.

ZACHARIAS WERNER (1768-1823), after the early death of his father, was reared by his eccentric mother, and remained all through his life a whimsical, unsteady man. He was religious, but frivolous, and a slave to his passions. He was fond of mysticism, and went over to the Catholic Church, but failed to find satisfaction there. His first drama was *Söhne des Thals* (Sons of the Valley) treating of the downfall of the order of Templars. While yet a Protestant, he wrote a tragedy on *Martin Luther, or the Consecration of Power.* One other play which made him quite prominent, but which at the same time prevented him from producing anything really lasting, was his fate-tragedy, *The Twenty-fourth of February* (a date supposed to be fruitful in mur-

Fate tragedies

derous deeds). It is remarkable as being the first of a whole deluge of fate-tragedies, which have haunted the German stage until very recent days. In them all Fate is presented as a malignant power, oppressing the guilty and the innocent alike. This was decidedly a step backward toward the old heathen idea of Fate, at the contemplation of which the mind stood terrified, and pitied the victims without being able to help them.

ECHOES OF ROMANTICISM

ADELBERT VON CHAMISSO (1781-1838) was a Frenchman by birth, but when he was only nine years old, his family were expelled from their country, and their estates confiscated. They went to Berlin, where the boy became attached to the land of his adoption. He entered the Prussian army, and did good service there until the war between Germany and France broke out, when he resigned his commission because he was unwilling to draw his sword against the land that gave him birth. From this time on he devoted much of his time to the study of the natural sciences, but while in retirement at the country-seat of a friend, he wrote, for his own diversion, and for the amusement of the children, his romantic story, *Peter Schlemihl.*

PETER SCHLEMIHL sells to the evil one, who appears to him in the form of a pleasing old man, his shadow for an inexhaustible bag of gold. But with his shadow, his peace is also gone; his wealth can not protect him from the scorn and contempt of men, who wish to have nothing to do with a man without a shadow. The possession of his lost shadow, however, he can obtain only by the forfeiture of his soul. Eternal salvation is of more importance to him than his earthly happiness, so he throws the purse away, and starts out through the world. By mere chance he finds a pair of seven-league boots, by the magic power of which he travels from place to place, and in this occupation finds peace and satisfaction.

The book was translated into all the languages of Europe, and there immediately arose numerous conjectures as to what the shadow might mean. The author maintained that it had no special meaning, but whether he was conscious of it or not, he did bring to beautiful poetical expression his sadness at having no fatherland.

Like the hero of his story he was restless, and in 1815 he joined an expedition to go around the earth. During three years consumed in scientific investigations in the various quarters of the globe, he came to think more and more of Germany, and when he returned, he became a German through and through. The University of Berlin honored him with the doctor's degree, and he was appointed director of the botanical garden. During the happiness of his home life he composed a beautiful group of poems under the title of *Frauenliebe und Leben* (Woman's Love and Life). In *Die alte Waschfrau* (Old Washerwoman) he gives a picture from among the common people, glorifying the faithful performance of duty, however menial it may be. His most complete work is *Salas y Gomez*. It was suggested by the sight of a precipitous and barren reef in the South Pacific, which the poet converted into the abode of a solitary ship-wrecked man, vainly waiting for relief. Chamisso's early poems were in harmony with the Romantic School, but he worked his way out of the vague ideas of that school into German simplicity and into real depth of thought.

JOSEPH BARON VON EICHENDORF (1788-1867) received his early education in Breslau, and then studied law in Halle, where, in addition to his professional studies, he occupied himself with poetry, especially that of the Romantic School. In Heidelberg, where he completed his law study, he associated with Clemens Brentano and Arnim, assisted them on *Des Knaben Wunderhorn*, and here published his first poems. He has been called the last knight of Romanticism. While he has much in common with that school, he rises high above them in the truth of feeling. After his university life, he returned to his father's home, and there assisted in the management of the large estate. During his quiet life at this time, arose many songs that are called the "ripest and most beautiful fruit of Romanticism."

He decided to begin his professional life in the service of the Austrian government, and had just passed the necessary examinations with great success when the Prussian call of 1813 for volunteers reached him, and he at once responded. He was in the army during the whole of the War of Liberation, and his patriotic songs written at this time are among the best in the language. In 1816 he entered on the practice of his profession, and gradually rose to high governmental positions. During all his professional life he was constantly engaged in literary work, and besides his poetry he has written numerous stories, the best known of which is probably his romantic "novelle," *Aus dem Leben eines Taugenichts* (Experiences from the Life of a Good-for-nothing), which in spite of its improbable adventures, with its light-hearted, singing, dreaming, musical hero, has remained a favorite.

The hero is a miller's son, who, with his fiddle starts out into the world. Two ladies whom he chances to meet are so delighted with his music that they take him with them to their castle. Through their influence he is made first gardener and then tax-gatherer, but he is not satisfied with his lot. Only one thing holds him, his love to the young countess, however hopeless it may be.

When he finally sees her in the company of a man whom he takes to be her betrothed, he gives up his position and travels farther into the world. After many adventures, he returns and learns that his loved one is not a countess at all, but the daughter of the old gate-keeper, and that she thinks of no one so much as of her Good-for-nothing.

CHAPTER XI

HEINRICH HEINE (1799-1856) was born at Düsseldorf, and was brought up as an orthodox Jew. He was destined for a commercial career, and was first sent to Frankfort to enter a banking establishment. This proving unsatisfactory, he went to Hamburg, and with the help of his rich uncle, set up a commission business that soon passed into liquidation.

His uncle, thinking that the boy was of little account, finally allowed him the means to go to the university. With the purpose of studying law, he went to Bonn and a year later to Göttingen, but he became more interested in the study of Old German literature and Indian poetry than he did in the dry formalism of law. He became attached to A. W. Schlegel, whom he in later years so shamefully ridiculed in his *Romantische Schule* (Romantic School). In 1821 he went to Berlin, and soon became intimate at the home of Varnhagen von Ense and his wife Rahel, people of culture and brilliant endowments, who regularly gathered about them the leading literary people of the city for the study of Goethe.

Education

In his first collection of poems (1822) he appears as the disciple of Romanticism, imitating the tones of the minnesong, and giving himself up to mystic influences of the Romantic School. Yet even in this first collection he frequently strikes a worthless and frivolous tone, which in his later development became so prevalent as to supersede entirely all traces of Romanticism. In 1825 he obtained the doctor's degree, and aspiring to a position in the employment of the government, he abjured the faith of his fathers, and was baptized into the Lutheran Church. This step was made from motives of expediency;

Change of Faith

HEINRICH HEINE

he had no faith in the doctrines of the church into which he was received, nor in the one from which he had come. Such abjurations were frequent, and were regarded by many as permissible, since only by so doing was a career open to them.

In the meantime the *Harzreise* (Hartz Journey), the fruit of his Göttingen student days, was completed and appeared in 1826 in the same volume with a collection of songs called *Heimkehr* (Return Home). Criticism was severe, but even the harshest critics were compelled to admire, and the general public were delighted with the pictures of the Hartz and the new chords of his poems of the sea. Many of the poems were at once set to music, and thus became popular. The *Harzreise* is probably the best known of his prose writings, and it is justly so, as he never surpassed it. During the same year appeared the first volume of the *Reisebilder* (Pictures of Travel), which was soon followed by three other volumes. These sketches, written in spirited yet often careless prose, and intermingled with poetry, soon found a public that was delighted with the arrogant scorn with which the author ridiculed the political and religious ideas of the times. The book opens with a satire on Göttingen student life, and then ridicules the heavy German erudition by the announcement of a learned disquisition on the subject of "The Feet of Göttingen Ladies," to be discussed under the following heads: Feet in general; feet of classical antiquity; feet of elephants; feet of Göttingen ladies; remarks about these feet in the student beer-gardens; these feet in their environment. Heine never tires of mocking Göttingen pedantry, and among other things tells of one professor's boy who would not play with another boy because he could not decline *mensa*. The most charming part of the book is probably the last part describing the Brocken, the students' spree on the top, and the descent of the mountain. The *Buch der Lieder* (Book of Songs, 1827) completely estab-

lished his fame. It contains some of the best he ever wrote,
and many of them are the best in the language. "Thou'rt
like a lovely floweret," "A lonely fir-tree standeth," and the
Lorelei are known and sung as folksongs all over Germany.

Character of poetry
Although many of his poems are the finest in
the realm of lyric poetry, only comparatively few
of them can be read without a tinge of disappointment. His brilliant wit was often distorted by cyni-
cism, and his frivolity frequently bordered on the insolent,
the vulgar, and even the obscene. In many of his writings
he arouses an intense emotion, and then spoils the effect of
it by some grotesque illusion. Heine was born in Germany,
and most of his works were written in German, but in mind,
in heart, and even in residence he was far from being a
German. His writings had become so hostile to the German
governments that he was finally declared an out-
An exile
law, and in 1831 he went to Paris, there to remain the rest of his unfortunate life.

Here he plunged into journalism, and into politics. He
wrote much on German topics for French readers, and never
failed to take advantage of an opportunity to ridicule the
land of his birth. In 1845 his writings were forbidden in
Germany, on account of their vicious religious and political
tendences. In 1841 he was legally married to MATHILDE
MIRAT, with whom he had been living for some six years,
and who tenderly loved the poet, and patiently waited on
him during his years of agony. In 1843 he visited Germany,
and then described his visit in *Deutschland, ein Winters-
märchen* (Germany, a Winter's Tale), a poem in which he
expresses, more strongly than before, his contempt for Germany and his hatred of Christianity. In much the same
strain, only more violent and more satirical, if such a thing
were possible, appeared in 1847 *Atta Troll, ein Sommer-
nachtstraum* (Atta Troll, a Summer Night's Dream).

Illness   Even now he was suffering from several nervous disorders, brought on largely by the excesses of his early life. His eyelids gradually became paralyzed, his vocal chords were affected, and a disease of the spinal marrow kept him a bedridden sufferer for a decade; an absolute wreck except in mind. The fortitude and patience with which he endured the pain and torture on his "mattress-tomb" win back our sympathy, which the scoffing cynic and wanton profligate of earlier days had well-nigh forfeited. We can not refuse to admire the strength of mind with which this poor wretch, paralyzed in his limbs, nearly deaf, eyes closed, propped up in mattresses on the floor,—he had long since been unable to lie in bed during his sleepless nights,—

Romancero   and amid paroxysms of pain, wrote the *Romancero* (1851). This book had a more rapid sale than any of his other works. Many of the poems are among his best. They show no sign of failing power, and many critics regard them as marking the height of his genius. Notwithstanding his sufferings, he continued to work as long as he could hear or speak at all, endeavoring to provide for his wife after he was gone. Thus he worked on until his death on the 17th of February, 1856.

Place in literature   Heine's place in literature has not yet been determined. Critics have tried to classify him, but the diversity of their classifications prove that the task is impossible. He himself knew not where he belonged. In the political and social world, he was somewhat like Goethe in the literary world. In the democratic upheaval of his time he saw more clearly than others the worthlessness of the long-established social and political institutions, but he had not the faintest idea of how to improve them. In early life he was a Romanticist, but later he was a realist in the extreme. He was in close touch with the "Zeitgeist," restless, questioning, and dissatisfied. He had broken loose from the old ethical moorings, and had secured no new ones. He is witty, his poems are clear, his satire keen, his songs are delicate and graceful, and they are among the best in German literature.

THEODOR KÖRNER

THE ERNST MORITZ ARNDT MONUMENT AT BONN, GERMANY

CHAPTER XII

POETS OF THE WAR OF LIBERATION

Condition of Germany Early in this century the old German Empire, founded by Charlemagne a thousand years before, passed out of existence; in 1807 Prussia was dismembered by the onward march of Napoleon, and then there followed seven years of humiliating subjection to the French tyrant. During this time many of the sons of Germany were awakening to the realization of their almost hopeless condition, and all over the country there were to be heard songs of patriotism, coming from pens known and unknown. SCHLEGEL, BRENTANO, EICHENDORF, FOUQUE, and KLEIST had written many a patriotic song. These and other causes had brought about a revival of national consciousness, and when the upheaval came in 1813, all classes joined in the enthusiasm. Philosophers, FICHTE in the lead, used their oratory to arouse the people, and the poets encouraged them with glowing war songs, which patriotic papers hastened to publish. The Romanticists were the first to sing of freedom and new national life, but a younger group arose who deserve to be called the poets of the war for freedom.

National awakening

MAX VON SCHENKENDORF (1783-1817) was born at Tilsit, studied law at Königsberg, and practiced there until 1812. During Prussia's humiliation he was so active in patriotic writing, that the approach of the French on their Russian campaign made it advisable for him to flee to southern Germany. In response to the royal proclamation he hastened to join the army against Napoleon. From this time on, every event in connection with the war resounded through his poems. From them we hear not so much the celebration of strife and of victory, as of the love of fatherland and of home; yet there is by no means a lack of poetic move-

ment in his war songs, and through them all there moves a
pious exaltation. Among the best of these are: *Landsturm-
lied* (Song of the Reserve) and *Soldatenmorgenlied* (Soldier's Morning Song).

After the battle of Leipzig he was introduced to the
leading officers of the army, his poems were printed and
distributed among the soldiers, and he was raised in rank.
At Napoleon's return from Elba, he uttered a warning in his
Frühlingsgruss an das Vaterland (Spring Greeting to the
Fatherland), announcing that still another struggle was before them. When the allied forces again occupied Paris,
he advised what came to Germany with the war of 1870-71
—the unification of Germany under the emperor. This
idea was so prevalent in his poems that RÜCKERT called him the *Emperor's Herald*. After the peace he wrote
still many a noble song: *Die deutschen Städte* (German
Cities), *Das Lied vom Rhein* (Song of the Rhine) and
Muttersprache (Mother Tongue). During his last years he
composed many spiritual songs full of feeling and sympathy.
In 1815 he was appointed government councilor at Coblenz,
and died there two years afterward.

THEODORE KÖRNER (1791-1813) will always remain one
of the interesting figures in the history and in the poetry
of the War of Liberation. He was the son of SCHILLER's
intimate friend, and grew up in admiration of the
poet who had been so closely connected with his home. He
began to write in imitation of Schiller, and for his songs
he frequently composed his own melodies. As a boy, he
played the violin, but soon gave that up for the guitar and his
lyre. He was skilled in drawing, in swimming, and in
fencing. Religious feeling permeated his life and poetry.
To give him some practical training, his father sent him to
a mining school, and later to the University of Leipzig, but
on account of some trouble growing out of a duel, he was
compelled to leave. He now went to Vienna, and devoted

himself to literature. He visited regularly the theater, wrote several comedies, which were warmly received, fell

Dramas in love with the actress ANTOINE ADAMBERGER, and soon was engaged to her. Under her influence he wrote *Zriny,* the drama that first gave him a reputation. He was appointed poet to the court theater, and a bright future seemed open for him. During his fifteen months' residence here, he wrote sixteen pieces for the stage, and although they were not all of high order, and most of them have been forgotten, they did fortell what activity was in store for Körner, had not an enemy's ball put an end to his life. While he was at the height of happiness, came the

As a soldier German call to arms; hard was the parting from his betrothed, but he hastened to join the Prussian army. For the service in the church, where the soldiers took the oath of allegiance, he composed the hymn. While marching toward Leipzig, under Major von Lützow, he wrote his celebrated song, *Lützows wilde Jagd* (Wild Chase). His heroic career from the time he entered the army in March until he was killed in August, 1813, is made immortal in his poems and songs, which his father published under the title of *Leier und Schwert* (Lyre and Sword), in 1814. Some of his poems worthy of especial mention are "The Call," "Quick, Up, My People! the Fire Signals are Smoking," *Gebet während der Schlacht* (Prayer during Battle), and *Das Schwertlied* (Sword Song). In a skirmish a few hours after he wrote the last one mentioned, he was struck by a ball; and when scarcely twenty-two years old, he gave up his life for the fatherland.

As a dramatist Körner is almost unknown, but his *Leier und Schwert* songs are familiar to the people. They sang them as they struggled against Napoleon in 1813, 1814, and 1815, and they sang them with the same vigor as they marched against Napoleon III in 1870 and 1871.

Far above the patriotic poets already mentioned, there

rose a man who from his eighteenth to his nineteenth birthday cultivated German song with remarkable vigor. This
was ERNST MORITZ ARNDT (1769-1860).

Education   Born on the island Rügen, he passed his boy-
              hood in humble surroundings, accustomed to
hard work and influenced by pious training. After meager
preparation he entered the University of Greifswald and
later went to Jena, to study theology. After his student days
he spent two years at home, teaching his brothers and sisters,
and preaching occasionally. Then followed extensive travel.
On his return he became instructor at the University of
Greifswald, five years later was promoted to a professorship,
and soon published the first part of his *Geist der Zeit* (Spirit
of the Age), which ran through Germany and was influential in arousing the national consciousness. On account of
              his bold addresses and writings, he became of-
During the   fensive to Napoleon. To avoid imprisonment
war   and possibly something worse, he went in 1806
to Stockholm, and remained three years in the service of the
Swedish government. Returning to Germany, he wandered
from place to place, sometimes under an assumed name, until
he was called by BARON VON STEIN as his secretary to St.
Petersburg, but a more important purpose was that he might
arouse, by his voice and his pen, the Germans living there.
There among other writings he published his *Katechismus
für den deutschen Kriegs- und Wehrmann* (Catechism for
the German Warrior), which was eagerly read from one end
of Germany to the other. His *Kriegs- und Wehrlieder*
(War Songs) from the years 1813 and 1814 went to the
hearts of the German people as no others ever did.

              After the war was over, he settled at Bonn, and
Professor-   built a house on the bank of the Rhine he loved
ship   so much, and in sight of the Seven Mountains.
Thither he soon brought as his wife the sister of the Berlin
preacher, SCHLEIERMACHER. In 1818 he was appointed pro-

fessor of history in the University of Bonn. No one was better fitted than he to lead young men; but he was not to be allowed to work on in quiet and ease. He was anxious that the people should reap the full advantage of the War of Liberation, and in the fourth part of his *Geist der Zeit,* which appeared about this time, some of the language was not pleasing to the government. Furthermore he was supposed to be connected with some movements that were not favored by the ruling power; his house was searched, his papers and letters taken, and the following year he was suspended from his position in the University. He was not idle, however, but during the twenty years that succeeded his discharge, he was busy with his pen, in the service of the fatherland and of the church. In *Vom Wort und vom Kirchenlied* (Church Songs), he pointed out the fine collection of hymns which had been produced during 300 years, and to this collection he added several that have found a permanent place in the hymn books of Germany. In 1840 King Friedrich William IV reinstated him in his former position, and did everything possible to make up for the injustice done him twenty years before. When in the same year the French threatened war, the old writer composed his "To the Rhine! Over the Rhine! All Germany forward into France!"[1]

Delegate from Frankfort Parliament
In 1848 he was elected to the Frankfort Parliament, and was one of the deputation sent to offer to Friedrich William IV the imperial crown. The refusal of the king to accept the honor grieved him, for he had long hoped to see Germany united under one central government. The rest of his life was spent in quiet retirement, yet his pen was active until the last, and he always hoped for what came to his country only ten years after his death—unification.

---

[1] The same occasion led Max Schneckenburger (1810-48) to write his *Die Wacht am Rhein* (Watch on the Rhine), which became during the campaign of 1870-71 the true national hymn of Germany.

FRIEDRICH RÜCKERT (1788-1866), who stands somewhat alone in German literature, deserves mention here, because he was interested in the war, and wrote numerous poems **Education** in connection with it. At the age of sixteen he entered the University of Würzburg to study law, but soon went to Jena, and devoted himself to the languages and literature; later he became instructor there. He desired to enter the campaign against the French, but his health forbade it, and he took up the cause the more strongly in his poetry. His *Deutsche Gedichte* (German Poems) ap- **War songs** peared in 1814, and among these were his *Geharnischte Sonette* (Sonnets in Armor). In spirited language he portrayed to the higher classes the shame and disgrace that had come upon them, and warned them to make every exertion in the struggle for existence. His *Kriegerische Spott—und Ehrenlieder* (War Songs of Disgrace and Honor) were intended for the masses, and they were warmly received. In other patriotic poems he complains of the ununited condition of Germany, and longs for the union of all the states in one strong central government. They are all permeated by an earnest, moral tone; they speak powerfully to the conscience, and praise German victories as the acts of God. *Auf die Leipziger Schlacht* (On the Battle of Leipzig) struck the popular tone as few other poems ever have done. For a few years after the war he resided in various places, devoting himself for the most part to the study of Oriental languages and literature.

Professorship In 1820 he settled in Coburg, which was practically his home during the rest of his life. Although he was soon called to the University of Erlangen, and later to Berlin as professor of Oriental languages, he still kept his country seat near Coburg, and retired thither whenever he could be absent from professional duties. As the first fruit of his study of the East, he published a collection of poems under the title of *Oestliche Rosen* (Oriental

Roses), much like Goethe's *Westöstlicher Divan*. *Lie-besfrühling* (Love's Springtime), containing many of the finest lyrics in the language, describes his love and court-ship, from the first meeting to the engagement. Rückert's poems are largely didactic; the best illustration of this is probably to be found in *Weisheit des Brahmanen* (Brahmin's Wisdom), a long collection written under the influence of his eastern study, but the contents of which is the expression of the poet's ideas about all possible realms of activity, art, science, poetry, etc. Some of his beautiful poems were oc-casioned by the death of his two youngest children, and it is characteristic of the poet that these *Kindertotenlieder* (Poems on the Death of my Children) remained in his desk, and were not published until after his death.

He had no love for public honor, even his professorship became a burden to him; and in 1848 he was released from it.

CHAPTER XIII

THE SWABIAN GROUP

Swabia, the section rich in a long course of history, and rich in literature, has produced a poet that won the hearts of his people as almost no one else has done in recent time, and who had the happy faculty of gathering around him a circle of literary friends, and leading them on to active independent work. This was LUDWIG UHLAND (1787-1862).

Born in Tübingen, where his grandfather had been professor of theology, and where his father was university secretary, he entered the University at the age of fifteen, to study law. His preference, however, was philology, especially the early German. The *Hildebranslied, and other* poems of the earlier times enlivened his poetic impulses, and aroused his desire for scientific investigation of the treasures of the earliest German literature. Of great importance was his circle of friends at the University, among whom was JUSTINUS KERNER, whose friendship he enjoyed for nearly sixty years. In 1810 he pasesd his examinations with high honor, received the degree of Doctor of Law, and a career in the legal profession stood open to him, but his heart was devoted to poetry. He went to Paris and there studied old French and German manuscripts, instead of French law and practice as his father had wished. After eight months he returned and was admitted to the bar. But this did not stop his work in poetry, and although he had at first been attached to the ideas of the Romantic School, he now devoted himself more to patriotic poetry.

Early interest in German literature

In 1812 he went to Stuttgart, soon entered politics, and became the leader of the party that for several years opposed the constitution offered by the king of Würtemberg. After this contest had somewhat subsided, he entered the legislative assembly, as a representa-

In politics

LUDWIG UHLAND

FRIEDRICH RÜCKERT

tive of Tübingen, and was always a supporter of the people. When not occupied with governmental work, he was busy with his studies in language and literature.

Professorship In 1830 came the appointment as professor of German language and literature at the University in Tübingen. He was warmly received by the students, and his rich store of knowledge made his lectures on German poetry of the Middle Ages very attractive. He was delighted with his new occupation, but was allowed to remain in it only three years. Being once more elected to the assembly, and being unable to secure a leave of absence from the University because he was opposed to the government, he resigned his professorship to accept the call that he regarded imperative. Six years he followed this call, and then refused re-election. His efforts had been largely in vain, and now the teaching profession was closed to him forever. He returned to Tübingen and devoted himself entirely to his literary work. His collection of German folksongs, even to-day regarded as a masterly, scholarly work, led him to make journeys to the north and south, and in all the large cities he was received with esteem and honor. Once more he came into public life as a member of the Frankfort Parliament, where he was strongly in favor of an elective central government, rather than an hereditary one.

Returning home he lived in retirement, wrapped up in his family, and his literary work. He was strong and active until a cold, which he caught while attending the funeral of his old friend Kerner, led to a sickness that carried him away on Nov. 13, 1862.

His works Uhland's poetry began with a romantic element, but he carefully avoided the errors of Romanticism. His songs are marked by simplicity and truthfulness, and they are so melodious and so musical that many of them —*Der Wirtin Töchterlein* (The Landlady's Daughter), *Der gute Kamerad* (The Good Comrade)—have become genuine and popular folksongs. The fundamental thought in them is always one of earnest morality and simple piety, and many of them contain a trait of fine and sound humor—*Die Kapelle* (The Chapel), *Schäfers Sonntagslied* (The Shepherd's Sunday-Song), *An die Unsichtbaren* (To the Invisible Ones), *Theelied* (Tea Song).

Ballads and romances   In his ballads and romances he has produced incomparable work. To the heroes of former days he has given new life and attractiveness. Among the best may be mentioned: *Das Schloss am Meer* (The Castle by the Sea), *Das Glück von Eden Hall* (The Luck of Eden Hall), *Des Goldschmieds Töchterlein* (The Goldsmith's Daughter), *Roland Schildträger* (Roland Shieldbearer), *Der Schwarze Ritter* (The Black Knight), and probably the best of all *Des Sängers Fluch* (The Minstrel's Curse), which caused commotion in Germany when it first appeared, because the bloody king was supposed to represent Napoleon.

Dramas   In the drama, also, Uhland has done work of real merit. Besides several incomplete drafts, we have two complete dramas *Ernst, Herzog von Schwaben* (Duke of Swabia), which treats of an old legend frequently used in literature, and *Ludwig, der Bayer* (The Bavarian), which treats of the struggle between Ludwig and Friedrich the Beautiful, of Austria, and of their reconciliation. German faithfulness is the theme of both dramas; in the first it is faithfulness toward a friend, while in the second, it is the faithful keeping of a promise.

JUSTINUS KERNER (1786-1862) was destined to a mercantile career, but found no delight in the calling, and through the assistance of an uncle entered the University in Tübingen as a student of medicine. Here he became acquainted with Uhland and Schwab, and in their company cultivated his love for poetry. After obtaining his degree, he spent some time in travel, and while in the neighborhood of

Heidelberg, composed one of his best poems, "Come, One More Drink of This Sparkling Wine."

Settling down to his profession, he gained an official appointment as chief physician in Weinsberg, where he lived until his death. The generous hospitality of his family and his interest in somnambulism and the spirit world, probably had as much to do with his fame as his poetry did. His home was open to everybody, and at all times. Poets and princes, and people from the lower walks of life, were his guests. The best of his poetry is in the form of songs and ballads, among which may be mentioned *Die Sägemühle* (The Sawmill), and *Der reichste Fürst* (The Richest Prince), and *Der Geiger von Gmünd* (The Fiddler at Gmünd).

Gustav Schwab (1792-1850) in his student days was an intimate friend of Kerner, and he called himself Uhland's oldest pupil. He published a collection of lyrics, and remodeled many of the old legends. Like Bodmer and Gleim he delighted to encourage young men of talent, and his home, like that of Kerner, was a meeting-place for poets. Among his best poems are *Der Ritter und der Bodensee* (The Knight and Lake Constance), *Das Mahl zu Heidelberg* (The Banquet at Heidelberg), and *Das Gewitter* (The Thunderstorm).

Wilhelm Hauff (1802-27), born in Stuttgart and educated in Tübingen, accomplished in his short life what led his countrymen to expect great things from him; he was frequently spoken of as the Walter Scott of Germany. Two of his poems have become folksongs: "When on the Midnight Watch I Stand," and "Dawning Day, Dawning Day, 'tis to Death You Light My Way." He is best known for the historical novel *Lichtenstein,* and for his charming "Novellen," among which may be mention *Das Bild des Kaisers* (The Emperor's Picture), *Phantasieen im Bremer Rathskeller* (Fancies in the Drinking-room of the Bremen City Hall), and *Die Bettlerin vom Pont des Arts* (The Beggar Girl of the Bridge of Arts).

EDUARD MÖRIKE (1804-75), a professor of German literature in Stuttgart, was successful in lyric poetry, although the number of his poems is small; some of them (e. g., *Das vergessene Mägdlein*) have become folksongs. His strong tendency to Romanticism appears in the novel *Maler Nolten*. *Mozart auf der Reise nach Prag* (Mozart on the Way to Prague) is an excellent "Novelle."

AUSTRIAN WRITERS.

Among the Austrian poets, benefited by the influence of the Romanticists, FRANZ GRILLPARZER (1791-1872) is the foremost. He lived a quiet and retired life, and not until toward the end of his career were appropriate praise and recognition bestowed upon him. He was a close student of German literature in all periods of its development, gained rich treasures from Goethe, learned much from Schiller and Shakespeare, and absorbed through the Romanticists inspiration from the Spanish writers. From all these sources he knew how to draw material and make it his own; and his greatest skill is probably in delicate and faithful psychological analysis. *Die Ahnfrau* (1817) was a fate-tragedy of the Romantic type. He next turned his attention to classic material and wrote *Sappho* (1818) and three years later *Das goldene Vliess* (Golden Fleece), a triology based on the Medea legend. He next chose a German historical theme and produced *Ottokars Glück und Ende* (King Ottokar, 1825), and this was followed by a romantic love-tragedy of Hero and Leander under the title of *Des Meeres und der Liebe Wellen* (Waves of the Sea and of Love). He has also left numerous proverbs and rich lyric poems.

FRIEDRICH HALM (1806-71), whose real name was MÜNCH-BELLINGHAUSEN, wrote several sensational dramas, of which three have obtained considerable fame: *Grisildis,* describing the cruel experiments by which Percival, a knight of the Round Table, tries the fidelity and devotion of his wife; *Der Sohn der Wildniss* (Son of the Wilderness), depicting the refining influence upon a savage by his love for a civilized captive girl; and *Der Fechter von Ravenna* (Swordsman of Ravenna), which is characterized by a warm, patriotic spirit, although it borders on sentimentality.

NIKOLAUS LENAU (1802-50), the German poet of sadness, was one of the great poets of Austria. His charming lyrics and short poems, many of them written during a year's sad wandering in America, and his epics *Savonarola* and *Faust* demonstrate poetic talent, that under happier circumstances might have placed him among the foremost singers of Europe.

ANASTASIUS GRÜN (1806-76), whose real name was GRAF VON AUERSPERG, after studying philosophy and law, traveled extensively, then settled down on his inherited estate, near Vienna. As a statesman he always strove for the advancement of his people, and his poetry is imbued with elevating political ideas. Especially is this true of *Spaziergänge eines Wiener Poeten* (Rambles of a Vienna Poet), and *Schutt* (Ruins), the latter describing the ruins of cities and empires, and contrasting the vanished glory of Venice and with the brilliant prospects of America. His epic *Letzter Ritter* (Last Knight) glorifies Emperor Maximilian I.

CHAPTER XIV.

RECENT AND CONTEMPORARY LITERATURE

National awakening In the productions of the patriotic poets of the first half of the century, may be seen a longing for political liberty and national unity. The first climax in this national development came with the effort that drove Napoleon from Germany in 1813; the same ideas grew continually, and came to a second outburst in the Revolution of 1848. After a short reaction from this unfortunate epoch, the same strivings again came to the front, and during the Franco-German war of 1870-71, led to the unification of Germany under the leadership of Prussia. The close student of Germany will see that these great political movements have been the outcome of the revolution in thought that began with Klopstock's *Messias*. He will also see that this revolution both in politics and literature is still going on, and that the final result is hidden in the future.

The Napoleonic wars, and the literature that grew up during and after them, were preparing Germany for a national uprising, and when the revolution in France dethroned Louis Philippe, the news flashed throughout Germany, and in most of the large cities there were revolutionary riots of more or less magnitude. Although suppressed, they convinced the governments of the necessity of numerous concessions. The Frankfort Parliament was called, and after long and heated discussions, King Friedrich William IV, of Prussia, was invited to become hereditary emperor. He declined the honor, the parliament was finally disbanded without any visible results, and it has too commonly been regarded as a failure, while in reality it was one of the most important events in Germany history. It was an effort, the result of a great national awakening;

without which the unification of Germany could never have been attained.

End of Classic-romantic art

In the meantime the Classic writers had brought German literature from its imperfection to high development; the Romanticists had woven into Classic literature, religious, patriotic, and historical elements; and the ideals of the Classic-romantic art were cultivated by a large number of gifted authors who brought it to its highest possible development. Heine and some of his followers tried in vain to change the long established literary tastes and principles; but the Revolution of 1848 was needed to bring the climax to the literary revolution that had long been struggling upward. With this year the great century of Classic-romantic art was closed. Even the external circumstances, periodicals, almanacs, and annuals, in which the readers had found their quiet æsthetic enjoyment, either disappeared, or lost their importance during the political storms of 1848-49. Although these storms led to a violent reaction, they awakened a lasting interest in civil, state, and national affairs. Mere æsthetic enjoyment and intellectual indulgence retreated into the background. Civil society became conscious of its interest in and its importance for public affairs. An earnest and active spirit arose and demonstrated that the object of art is not merely to adorn life with its charms, but that it is the expression and representation of the whole human life in all its phenomena. Thus gradually new principles gained the ascendency, and chief among these was that art must always stand in close relation to reality. Lyric and epic poetry gradually yielded to those types of literary art that best represent life in its many phases, especially the drama and the novel.

New principles

Although this epoch produced no Goethe or Schiller, and although literature had yielded to politics and statesmanship as a national motive power, and although generals

13

and statesmen were far more evident than thinkers and poets, yet there were large numbers of literary men of sturdy respectability, deep thinkers, genuine patriots, whose productions are sure to last.

EPIC AND LYRIC POETS.

HOFFMANN VON FALLERSLEBEN (1798-1874), after having studied literature and philology at Göttingen, was appointed professor at the university in Breslau, but some seven years later was compelled to give up his position on account of political hostility engendered by his *Unpolitische Lieder* (Nonpolitical Poems). After years of wandering he was called as librarian to the monastery in Corvey, where he lived until his death. His political poetry has long been forgotten, but he was the author of a large number of popular musical poems in which he touched all the tones of lyric poetry, and which have found a warm place in the hearts of his countrymen. The most loved of all is the patriotic song: *Deutschland, Deutschland, über Alles.* His joy at the return of spring and his delight in travel he has expressed in many a poem; love poems and children's songs from his pen are numerous; and he has done real scholarly service in the publication of poetry from the Old High German period.

FERDINAND FREILIGRATH (1810-76) was destined, against his will, to the career of a merchant, and his education was consequently interrupted at an early stage. His first collection of poems met with such a warm reception that he gave up the uncongenial calling, and devoted himself to writing. The revolutionary tendency of his poetry during the forties compelled him to flee to England, where he remained for the most part until 1868. His return was a signal of rejoicing, and to the poet, who had grown gray in exile, and whose finances were exhausted, a handsome welcome was extended in the shape of a purse of over $40,000, contributed by his friends in Europe and in America. He was truly a German, and entered into every German project with all his heart.

There are two quite different sides to his poetry: one develops with luxuriant coloring and wonderful clearness pictures from foreign lands; the other presents a series of thoughtful German poems, which rank with the finest that Germany has. As belonging to the first class might be mentioned: *Der Löwenritt* (Lion Ride), *Das Gesicht des Reisenden* (Face of the Traveler), *Der Mohrenfürst* (Prince of the Moors); to the second class, *Die Tanne* (Fir Tree), *Die Auswanderer* (Emigrants), *Die Bilderbibel* (Picture Bible), and *Ruhe in der Geliebten* (Rest with One's Love). His pen was busy during the war of 1870-71; when the French made their declaration, he greeted it with the rousing hymn *Hurra Germania,* and then with a poetical blessing sent his eldest son as a volunteer. To the memory of the heroes who fell, he dedicated his ballad, *Die Trompete von Gravelotte.*

As a translator of French and English poetry, Freiligrath stands unsurpassed. He has taken the poems of Robert Burns to the German people, and his translation of the *Song of Hiawatha,* by Longfellow, who was an intimate friend of his and who tried to bring the exiled poet to America, is a masterly piece of translation.

EMANUEL GEIBEL (1815-84) was in his early studies a good scholar and very skillful in handling music and poetry. He entered the University of Bonn to study theology and philology, but soon went to Berlin and devoted himself to the classics. Most of his evenings he spent in some of the finest families of the city, especially at the homes of Chamisso and Bettina von Arnim, the latter of whom succeeded in helping him to a position as private tutor in Athens, whither the young man went and spent much time in wandering through the renowned places of antiquity. Returning to Germany in 1840, he published the first collection of his poems, which at first did not meet with the approval of the critics, but which gradually won their way into favor. Their popularity is attested not merely by the fact that they had passed through one hundred editions by the time he died, but also by the delight with which they are sung in social gatherings, in the workshop, and by the students. The favor of the Prussian king, by granting him a small annuity for life, put him in a position to devote himself more completely to poetry. In 1852, the king of Bavaria called him as honorary professor to the university in Munich. Although financially insignificant, his position was one of honor and pleasure; in the winter he lectured on German literature and æsthetics, and spent the summer as he chose. But his home and heart were in the North, and his patriotic wish was to see Germany united under the scepter of the king of Prussia. The expression of this desire aroused some jealousy in the royal family in Munich, and his position soon became unattractive. With little regret he returned to his native city, where he had the satisfaction of seeing his boldest dreams realized in the unification of Germany.

Geibel is the foremost lyric poet since Goethe and Heine. Among some of the best known of his poems may be mentioned: "O Hasten, My Horse, Be Quick, Be Quick," "May Has Come, the Trees Are Budding," "When Two Hearts Separate." His patriotic poetry, strong and energetic, has been collected under the title, *Heroldsrufe* (Herald's Cry). From 1840 to 1871, he took an active part in all the steps in the development of the empire, and his poetry had no small influence in bringing about the result. The fundamental tone in these poems is warm love for the fatherland and a pious Christian faith. He has done good work in epic poetry, but even in this the lyric element is often introduced, especially so in *König Sigurds Brautfahrt* (King Sigurd's Bridal Trip). As a writer of drama, too, Geibel will always be remembered.

His most successful effort in this line is *Brunhild* (1857) in which he tries to bring the personages of the old epic nearer to our understanding by representing them as they probably were before they came under the influences of Christianity.

During a previous visit to Isenstein, SIEGFRIED has aroused in the heart of the heroic maiden a passionate love for him, yet without suspecting it. Anxiously and with deep longing, she waits for his return, and for his sake she frightens away all other wooers by the dreaded athletic contests. From these circumstances it is readily seen why, when she learns how both he and GUNTHER have deceived her, her love is turned to hatred, and why she never rests until Siegfried lies dead at her feet. That she may be with him in the other world, she falls on his sword, crying: "You have gone before, I follow—receive me."

Sophonisbe, his next drama, is written in noble language, and is admirably arranged, but it has never been popular on the stage.

GOTTFRIED KINKEL (1815-82), after completing his theological studies, began lecturing on church history at Bonn, and at the same time served as assistant pastor of the evangelical church at Cologne. Seven years later he was appointed professor of the history of art, but could devote only two years to this work, as the troubles of 1848 carried him from his study into the active field of politics. He entered the democratic cause, joined the revolutionary party in Baden, was soon captured and cast into prison at Spandau. With the help of his friend, Carl Schurz, whom political oppression drove to America, he escaped in 1850 to England, where he soon found a position in London as professor of German literature. After sixteen years of exile he returned to German-speaking people, but not to Germany. He passed the rest of his life as a professor in the Polytechnic in Zurich. In his poetry, which is comparatively free from political tendencies, the epic element prevails. *Bilder aus Welt und Vorzeit* (Pictures from the Past) are ballads presenting the forms of Theodoric, Brunhild, Cæsar, and others. For *Otto der Schütz* (Otto the Marksman), written somewhat after the manner of the old German epics, he chose his material from one of the old Rhine legends. He has been successful in the lyric, but the best of this class were probably those written before his political difficulties. The songs of his exile breathe a deep longing for his home in the Rhineland, and they are full of ardent wishes for the unity and greatness of the German people.

OSKAR VON REDWITZ (1823-91) owes his first renown to his romantic poem *Amaranth,* which, appearing soon after the disturbances of 1848, lauds the church and royalty, and stigmatizes the Liberals as subverters of peace and order. After giving expression to the Catholic *tendenz* in a few other works (among them the drama *Sigilinde*) he freed himself largely from this influence, and with patriotic enthusiasm celebrated the struggle of 1870-71 in his *Lied vom neuen deutschen Reich* (Song of the New German Empire). At the age of fifty he wrote the epic *Odilo,* which is filled with a more modern Christian spirit than his earlier works. Among his dramas the best are *Philippine Welser* and *Der Zunftmeister von Nüruberg.*

OTTO ROQUETTE (1824-96) began his literary career with *Waldmeisters Brautfahrt* (Waldmeister's Bridal Trip), which he calls a Rhine, Wine, and Wandering story. It came at a time when the people were tired of political writings, and it soon won favor. Although written in epic form, it owes much of its popularity to the lyric charm and the rollicking fun pervading the entire poem. It is the story of the marriage of Prince Waldmeister, who, with the aid of his servants, escapes from a botanizing-box. Twenty-five years later a sequel, *Rebenkranz zu Waldmeisters silberner Hochzeit* (Vine Garland to Waldmeister's Silver Wedding), also became popular. His best novels are *Buchstabierbuch der Leidenschaft* (Spelling Book of Passion) and *Im Hause der Väter* (In the Home of our Ancestors). Into many of his stories he has woven episodes and characters of history; as examples may be mentioned *Grosse und kleine Leute in Alt-Weimar* (Great and Little People in old Weimar), and *Der gefrorene Kuss* (The Frozen Kiss), one of the leading characters in which is Goethe. He wrote several dramas that have been presented on the leading stages of Germany.

JOSEPH VICTOR VON SCHEFFEL (1826-86), after thorough preparation for law, practiced his profession for a few years, and then went to Italy determined to become an artist, but whether painter or poet he could not tell. Unable to decide, he went to the island of Capri, there to make his decision in solitude. The popularity of his first poem, *Trompeter von Säkkingen,* proves beyond a doubt that he made no mistake as to his calling.

At the time of the Thirty Years' War, YOUNG WERNER, a student at Heidelberg, is expelled because when intoxicated, he has declared in languishing verse his love for the Princess LEONORE. With his trumpet, which he can handle with masterly skill, he starts for a journey through the Black Forest. At a feast he sees MARGARETA, the daughter of Baron Säkkingen, and at once love's magic seizes him. He enters her father's service as trumpeter, and wins his favor, especially by defending the castle against the peasants. He is wounded, but Margareta's care saves him; the convalescence leads to a mutual declaration of love; but the baron objects to the marriage. Once more young Werner begins his wanderings, and after many an adventure, arrives in Rome, and becomes the pope's chorister. Margareta, who is almost dying of a broken heart is sent to Rome for a change of air; here she sees her lover, the pope learns of their love, raises Werner to the rank of a knight, and blesses their union. Much excellent humor and many a charming song are woven into the poem.

On his return Scheffel lived in Heidelberg, among a jovial company of lovers of poetry and song. In 1867 he gathered his poems together, and published them under the title of *Gaudeamus*. An earnest lyric tone is prevalent in his collection *Frau Aventiure*, which owes its existence to a visit he paid to the Wartburg, and more especially to the impression made upon him by the painting of the legendary "Sängerkrieg." His greatest work, however, was done in the historical novel *Ekkehard*. In rather quaint and archaic language, Scheffel tells of the love of the young monk Ekkehard, to the Duchess Hadwig, of Swabia.

According to an old chronicle, the DUCHESS had invited the MONK to her home merely for the sake of his learning, and had tormented him by her whims, without having any other feeling for him. Later on, at the recommendation of the duchess, he was received at the imperial court, where he lived long in high honor. In Scheffel's poem, the monk's passionate love leads him to so far forget himself as to embrace and kiss the duchess in the chapel. Seen by hostile monks, he is confined, but escapes, and then lives as a hermit, gradually coming to peace and rest, and finding consolation in poetry. Having written the *Waltarilied,* he binds it to an arrow and sends it to his loved one. As it falls at the feet of the duchess, and as she reads the inscription, "A Parting Greeting to the Duchess of Swabia," and also the proverb of the apostle, "Blessed is the man who endureth temptation,"—the proud woman bows her head and weeps.

His characters are skillfully drawn, his works abound in genuine German humor, and he has succeeded wonderfully well in using an archaic language. He is unquestionably one of the most popular men in the whole range of German literature, a fact demonstrated by the ovation given him by the people on his fiftieth birthday. Quite a number have imitated him, and among those who have more or less closely been his disciples, may be mentioned WEBER, WOLFF, and BAUMBACH.

FRIEDRICH WILHELM WEBER (1813-94), after spending the most of his life in the practice of medicine, partly retired, and withdrew to a secluded home. After translating

several poems from Tennyson, he published in 1878 his epic
Dreizehnlinden, which at once became popular. The action
of the poem takes place in old Saxony in the ninth century,
and represents the last struggle of the heathen Saxons
against forcible conversion under Charlemange, and the
final victory of Christianity. Among his smaller poems
are to be found many a gem in lyric and in ballad. The
scene of *Goliath* (1892) is laid in Norway, and is based on
a true episode. The hero is reared in the home of a rich
peasant, and when he becomes bold enough to sue for the
peasant's daughter, the father turns him out of the house.
The young people remain true to each other, and also bow
in obedience to parental authority. The peasant dies un-
reconciled, the daughter informs her lover of this fact,
but both honor her father's command. She visits him once
a year for a "summer day," and the rest of their lives is
spent in the peace and quiet of renunciation.

JULIUS WOLFF (born at Quedlinburg, 1834, now in Berlin) quickly became popular through his numerous short
epics, in which he revived the legends of bygone days.
Till Eulenspiegel resembles the famous jester of the
fifteenth century in little more than name; *Der wilde Jäger*
(Wild Huntsman), refers to the wild huntsman of Bürger's
ballad; and *Der Rattenfänger von Hameln* (Rat-catcher
of Hameln), treats of the player who freed Hameln from
the rats, claiming as his reward a kiss from the burgo-
master's daughter. The refusal, and his imprisonment, lead
him to take vengeance by enticing all the girls of the town
to a neighboring hill, where they disappear. In *Tann-
häuser,* which Wolff calls a minnesong, but which might
better be called a historical novel in verse, he identifies
the minnesinger of this name with the legendary Heinrich
von Ofterdingen, and surrounds him with numerous well-
known minnesingers. *Lurlei* (1886), treats of the well-
known Rhine legend, and attributes the dangerous incanta-

tions of the beautiful rock-demon to the vengeful spirit of a water-sprite who seeks to entice and kill men indiscriminately, in revenge for having been deserted by the knight of Katzenelnbogen. *Die Pappenheimer* (1889), in which he gives a somewhat offensive picture of the plundering of the Thirty Years' War, rather moderated the enthusiasm of his admirers. In *Renata* (1891) he returns to his former style, and celebrates the victory of the Renaissance over the antique in art. The addition of *Der fliegende Hollender* (Flying Dutchman, 1892), *Assalide* (1896), in which he gives a picture of troubadour life in southern France, and *Der Landknecht von Cochem* (1898) easily make him the most prolific of modern epic writers, as he is also probably the most successful. A few dramas among his early works have proved almost a failure, but his novels have been quite popular, especially *Der Sülfmeister* (Saltmaster), which describes the independence of the old city of Lüneburg in warding off the domineering influence of the clergy and the duke, and *Das schwarze Weib* (Black Woman).

RUDOLF BAUMBACH (1841, now at Meiningen) has gained a worthy place in both lyric and epic poetry. His *Lieder eines fahrenden* Gesellen (Ballads of a Wanderer) are filled with charming and natural freshness, accompanied by light and pleasing humor. He was a great traveler, and many of his poems owe their charm to the influences of his wanderings. His joy in life, and in the beauty of the world permeates the collection *Thüringer Lieder* (Songs of Thuringia). His best epics are *Horand und Hilde,* a free treatment of the Gudrun legend and *Frau Holde,* the fundamental idea of which is that true love, severely tried, is always rewarded.

WILHELM JORDAN (1819, now living at Frankfort) has probably done his greatest service to German literature in popularizing the Nibelung legend. His great poem *Nibelunge,* which he read in public all over Germany, differs in both matter and form from the epic of the Middle Ages. Jordan goes back to the earlier ballads and songs, and molds his poem, just as the epoch is supposed to have arisen. He uses alliterative verse, and avoids much of the bloodshed and many of the horrors of the old poem. Although there is much in his production that is modern and rhetorical, yet it has done good service in acquainting the Germans of to-day with their early literature. He has lately given attention to the drama and the novel. The best of the former are *Durch's Ohr* (Through the Ear), *Zwillingsbruder* (Twin Brother), and *Liebesleugner;* and of the latter *Die Sebalds* and *Zwie Wiegen* (Two Cradles). His translations of the *Iliad* and the *Odyssey* are works of the first order.

THEODORE FONTANE (1819-98) is probably best known for his patriotic writings. His poetry came to its fullest development during the wars of 1864, 1866, 1870. Several years' residence in Scotland and England led him to write a series of ballads based on the legends he found there. In 1878 he published his first novel, *Vor dem Sturm* (Before the Storm), in which he characterizes the gloomy threatening time of the winter of 1812-13. He is also quite successful in the short story (e. g., *Grete Minde* and *Ellernklipp*). More recently he has written several novels dealing with phases of Berlin life.

Among the numerous women who have cultivated poetry, the most important is doubtless ANNETTE VON DROSTE-HÜLSHOFF (1797-1848). Her poetry is largely narrative in nature, sometimes strong and manly in tone, and sometimes stamped with truly womanly character. Many of her productions abound in fresh and healthy humor. Her own inner life is expressed in *Das Geistliche Jahr,* which consists of poems for every Sunday and feast-day in the Catholic calendar, and shows the severe struggles through which she passed before she attained spiritual peace.

CHAPTER XV.

NOVELISTS.

In Germany, as in the whole modern world, the most popular literary production is the novel. In it the author is permitted to discuss all the interesting questions of the present time, or his purpose may be simply to entertain. Most authors, however, use the novel as a means of promulgating their ideas in regard to subjects in which they are interested, and in the whole range of literature these subjects are very numerous: history, philosophy, pedagogy, religion, and political and social matters. Goethe was the first man in Germany to make use of this new form of literature, and his *Werthers Leiden, Wilhelm Meister,* and *Wahlverwantschaften* have not yet ceased to be imitated. Under the influence of newly awakened national consciousness, and as a complement of national development, the historical novel, seeking its material in past historical events and personages, has been extensively cultivated in Germany. Among the large number of those who have written such novels, the following may justly be regarded as the most successful: ALEXIS, SCHEFFEL (Ekkehard), FREYTAG, DAHN, EBERS, MEYERS, and RIEL.

THE HISTORICAL NOVEL.

WILIBALD ALEXIS (1798-1871), whose real name was WILHELM HÄRING, produced in imitation of Walter Scott a series of historical novels, dealing largely with Prussian events and all filled with newly awakened patriotism. Frederick the Great and his Career, is the subject of *Cabanis.* Alexis may be regarded as the founder of the historical novel in Germany.

GUSTAV FREYTAG (1816-95) studied the German language and literature at the Universities in Breslau and Berlin, and

From a Photograph by Karl Schipper, Wiesbaden

GUSTAV FREYTAG

From a Photograph by George Brokesch, Leipzig

GEORG EBERS

later became an instructor at the University in Breslau, but soon gave up teaching and turned his attention to dramatic poetry. Several of his pieces met with great success, especially the comedy *Die Journalisten*. He obtained a lasting success in his novel *Soll und Haben* (Debit and Credit), in which he treats in a realistic manner the restless labor of the commercial class, weaving into the story representatives of the farming and industrial classes. In *Die verlorene Handschrift* (Lost Manuscript) he has represented the rather overdrawn conflict between the scholarly circle and the society of the court. At the same time he had continued his study of history, and from this study he was led to the production of *Bilder aus der deutschen Vergangenheit* (Pictures of German Life). These pictures begin at the origins of German history, and extend down to modern times. They present, not the political history of Germany, but rather the history of German civilization. Closely connected with, and growing partly from, this great work, is his group of novels under the title of *Die Ahnen* (Forefathers). This national epic in the form of a novel is composed of eight parts and describes numerous events in the development of a single race from the time of the barbaric migrations down to the present time. Most of the events are presented as taking place in the land of Thuringia.

FELIX DAHN (1834, now professor in Breslau) gave to his first novel the title *Ein Kampf um Rom* (Fight for Rome), in which he represents the struggle and downfall of the East Gothic kingdom in Italy. To the times of the barbaric migrations he has devoted several novels, one of which, *Felicitas*, is located in Salzburg, in the eventful year of 476. In describing the struggle between the Romans and the Germans, he has drawn a marked contrast between the fresh and noble heroes of the North and the morally benumbed and degenerate men of the South. In *Nordische Romanen* (Novels of the North), he treats of the mythology of the early Germans. *Die schlimmen Nonnen von Poitiers* (Naughty Nuns of Poitiers) describes an isolated event of the year 589, but it is a story which, with a few changes, might be made to represent events in a girls' school of modern times. He has also tried his hand in the drama, and his *König Roderick* represents this last king of the Goths as a firm character, stoutly defending the state from encroachments by the church; while *Rüdiger von Bechlaren* has for its background the character in the Nibelungenlied.

GEORGE EBERS (1837-98) has devoted much time to the study of Egypt and her hieroglyphics, and he delights to make that country the scene of his novels. He made several journeys there, and on one of his trips he discovered the valuable papyrus that has been named after him. His first novel is *Eine ägyptische Königstochter* (Egyptian Princess). The heroine is the daughter of King Amasis. *Uarda* portrays the brilliant period of the Ptolemies under King Rameses; *Die Schwestern* (Sisters) carries the reader back to the year 64 B. C., and is located in Memphis, now at the temple of Serapis, now at the castle of the Ptolemies; *Der Kaiser,* in which the heroes are Hadrian and his favorite Antonius, is laid in Alexandria, midway between the East and West, and shows how Christianity made its way into the king's home. In *Frau Bürgermeisterin* (Mayor's Wife) he chose to return to a land nearer home, and has given us a thrilling tale of the Siege of Leyden, 1574. The faithful woman keeps up the courage of the besieged until the long-looked-for help comes. *Ein Wort* is the story of a simple-minded youth who starts in search of the one word that will harmonize all existence, and finally finds it to be "love." *Cleopatra* is more academic than any of its predecessors, and is so overloaded with wearisome and irrelevant detail as to make the book very unattractive to the ordinary reader.

By far the larger number of Eber's novels are laid in the

East, but in recent years he has turned his attention to the Germany of the Middle Ages, and especially to the old city of Nuremberg, a place that has always interested him from the time of his boyhood. *Die Gred* (1888) and *Im Schmiedefeur* (In the Fire of the Forge, 1894) are genuine historical pictures of Nuremberg life from the fifteenth and thirteenth centuries respectfully. *Im blauen Hecht* (In the Blue Pike, 1895), the name of a small inn, is not located in the city of Nuremberg, but in that neighborhood, and some of the characters are Nuremberg people. *Barbara Blomberg* (1896), although German in character, is rather a psychological than a historical novel. It marks quite a change in the author's method, and classes him with the realistic school. In *Arachne* (1897) the author returns once more to Egyptian life, taking his readers among the weavers of the Nile Delta, to Alexandria and the art-loving Pergamos.

CONRAD FERDINAND MEYER (1825-98) has been a much less prolific writer than those just discussed, but his historical tales are among the best in German. The hero of *Jürg Jenatsch* is one of the most interesting and puzzling characters in Swiss history during the Thirty Years' War. *Das Amulett* contains the experiences of two young men of Switzerland, during the horrors of the night of St. Bartholomew, in Paris. *Der Heilige* (Thomas à Becket) carries the reader into the midst of the struggle between the secular powers and the pope during the Crusades. *Die Versuchung des Pescara* and *Angela Borgia,* both located in Italy, are written with masterly skill. Among his poems *Huttens letzte Tage* (Huten's Last Days) is probably the best.

WILHELM HEINRICH RIEHL (1823-97) is the author of a large number of "Novellen," the best of which deal with events of importance in the development of Germany. The collections *Kulturgeschichtliche Novellen* and *Geschichten aus alter Zeit* are among the best known.

THE NOVEL OF CONTEMPORARY LIFE.

Far more popular than the historical novel, and cultivated by whole armies of writers, is the novel of contemporary life. It is almost always a novel of purpose, and will seldom give to succeeding generations an impartial and faithful picture of the social, political, and religious questions of our time. The leaders in this kind of literature are FREYTAG (*Soll und Haben, Die verlorene Handschrift*), GUTZKOW, SPIELHAGEN, HEYSE, KELLER, STORM, and WILDENBRUCH.

KARL GUTZKOW (1811-78) published *Die Ritter vom Geist* (Knights of the Spirit) and *Der Zauberer von Rom* (Sorcerer of Rome), each in nine volumes. In the first he wished to represent to younger generations the reaction of 1849-50. The second discusses German Catholicism, and advocates a religion free from Rome.

FRIEDRICK SPIELHAGEN (1829, now in Berlin), established his reputation by *Problematische Naturen* (Problematic Characters), which is continued and completed in *Durch Nacht zum Licht* (Through Night to Light). With keen power of observation he has developed characteristic portraits from modern society, but, for the most part, they are somewhat one-sided. Especially is his prejudice toward the artistocracy and the clergy apt to allow only hypocrites or fools to appear in his novels as representatives of these classes. In the succeeding novels, *Die von Hohenstein, In Reih und Glied* (Rank and File), *Hammer und Amboss* (Hammer and Anvil), this tendency is still more prevalent. In *Sturmfluth* (Breaking of the Storm), however, he portrays a Prussian general and nobleman of cultured character, without any one-sided development; and the clergy are kindly treated. From an artistic standpoint this novel marks the highest point in Spielhagen's writing, and the excellent thought of comparing the storm of the elements with the

From a Photograph by Jos. Albert

PAUL HEYSE

From a photograph by Loescher & Petsch, Berlin

ERNST VON WILDENBRUCH

commotion in society brought about by the results of the war with France, is carried through with a masterly hand.

Besides his novels Spielhagen composed numerous "Novellen," among which may be mentioned: *Was die Schwalbe Sang* (What the Swallow Sang), *Die Dorfkokette* (The Village Coquette), *Ultimo,* and *Quisisana,* which describes the sad heart history of a cultured, elderly man. With great skill, and at the very beginning, the right chords are struck, and the gentle tones sound through all the happy and serious scenes like the music of a delicate harp. In many of the author's novels there is a heavy element of fate which crushes everybody in its way. *Susi* (1895) fortunately quite free from this, is one of his best shorter novels. It is a realistic picture of the corrupt morals of a court, the original of which exists, only too numerously. In the drama, too, he has tried his skill, but with only mediocre success. His talent is at its best in the field of the great social novel. He stands high above all others in depicting the surging of the masses, and the swaying of party strife at the present time.

PAUL HEYSE (1830, now in Munich) is beyond comparison the greatest master in the "Novelle," which in his hands has been brought almost to artistic perfection. His psychological problems are completely and clearly demonstrated, and his catastrophies are quickly and vividly developed. Most of them are love stories, which are frequently carried through peculiar and adventuresome scenes. The characters are for the most part of noble physical beauty, and refined demeanor; the hateful and ugly is distasteful to Heyse. His portraiture of charming women is so nearly perfect that he has chosen women for the chief characters of most of his "Novellen." *L'Arrabbiata* is a romantic love story located on and near the Bay of Naples. *Das Glück von Rothenburg* (The Fortune of Rothenburg) describes in a congenial manner the victory of a noble German housewife over a fashionable and coquettish foreigner.

14

Unfortunately there appears in many of his works the fruit of his atheistic and pessimistic ideas, which come to a more complete expression in *Kinder der Welt* (Children of the World). This may be called a triumph-song of the children of the world over the children of God. The same ideas are prevalent in *Im Paradiese,* which derives its name from the artists' quarter in Munich, and which describes the rather questionable morals and life of the painters and sculptors. *Der Roman der Stiftdame* (Romance of the Canoness, 1886) is free from pessimism and presents a realistic and thrilling picture of life. *Ueber allen Gipfeln* (Above the Tree-tops, 1895) is a novel abounding in several well-arranged plots, whose characters stand out before the reader as though they were in flesh and blood. Three stories published during 1896 have been widely read: *Das Rätsel des Lebens* (Problems of Life), *Verrathenes Glück,* and *Abenteuer eines Blaustrümpfchens* (Adventure of a Bluestocking), the scene of the last being laid in Munich and depicting the experiences of an incomprehensibly naïve woman from a small town, as she seeks the society and influence of artists and literary people. Numerous other stories continue to appear, to the delight of Heyse's admirers.

In lyric poetry and in the drama, Heyse has produced considerable work of real value, but his success in these lines is far from being up to that in the novel.

GOTTFRIED KELLER (1815-90) chose for his first novel *Der grüne Heinrich* (Green Henry), the story of his own life. *Die Leute von Seldwyla* (The People of Seldwyla), a "Novelle," is a realistic and yet ideal picture of village life. In the *Zürich Novellen* he has related the history of his native city from the time of the minnesingers. This work met with great success, and the interest aroused by it called attention to the earlier works, which had not been very warmly received. In his last group of "Novellen," under the title of *Sinngedicht* he has treated from various standpoints the same subject; namely, the choice of a husband or a wife. Here he has shown a preference for modern circumstances, and has pictured them in their ethical and poetical relations.

THEODORE STORM (1817-88) rivals Heyse as a writer of short stories, although his legal profession occupied much of his time and prevented him from producing a large amount of literature. His first story, *Immensee* (1850), has remained the most characteristic and most popular. Here, as in many others, he shows his art of influencing his readers more by what he does not say than by what he does. *Abseits* and *Unter dem Tannenbaum* (Under the Fir-tree) express the grief of his countrymen at the foreign control of their home. *Späte Rosen* and *Veroneika* present psychological problems from married life, and *Viola tricolar*, based on his own experiences, treats of second marriage. *Psyche*, bright and cheerful, is regarded by many as his best. *Beim Vetter Christian* (At Cousin Christian's) is a good picture of German home life. His later stories, among them *Aquis submersus, Carsten Curator*, and *Der Schimmelreiter*, are overshadowed by melancholy or tragic features. They are based on events in past history, and are good historical novels.

ERNEST VON WILDENBRUCH (1845, now in Berlin), although best known as a dramatist, has written several excellent novels and " Novellen," and they are of special value because they are based on his own personal experiences. The first "Novelle," *Der Meister von Tanagra*, describes his own artistic development. The theme of most of his novels is the winning or conquering of a strong, original, or refined woman by a man, generally an artistic genius. Before the woman yields there is a long, hard struggle, for stern pride and quiet self-control is a fundamental characteristic of nearly all his women, and these must be overcome before the heart of the strong, self-reliant woman melts and returns the passion of the man. In *Eifernde Liebe* (Zealous Love, 1893) the struggle is complete, but leads to a tragic end, while *Schwester-Seele* (Sister-souls, 1894) leads to a happy conclusion. These are his two great novels, but the same theme in one variation or another appears in his shorter stories, among which should be mentioned: *Francesca von Rimini, Der Astronom, Vor den Schranken* (Before the Bar) and *Hexenliede* (Witch's Song), the last two based on Wildenbruch's experiences as a lawyer, *Die Danaide,* which, with the Franco-German War as a background, portrays the struggle of a woman in love with an enemy of her country, and *Kinderthränen,* a collection showing where earthly happiness is to be found.

When the Swiss pedagogue PESTALOZZI (1746-1827) published his *Lienhard und Gertrud,* he introduced into German literature a new kind of novel, which has developed into the class of stories known as " Village Tales." Of the numerous writers that have cultivated this kind of literature, by far the most famous is BERTHOLD AUERBACH (1812-82). He was a village boy, born of Jewish parents in the Black Forest, where he passed most of his childhood, and whither he always delighted to return. His education was begun in one of the leading Jewish schools, but becoming tired of the narrow circle of the rabbinical studies, he entered the University, began the study of law, and soon became interested in philosophy.

His first work was *Spinoza,* a novel in which he glorifies his favorite philosopher and his pantheistic doctrines. His *Schwarzwälder Dorfgeschichten* (Village Tales of the Black Forest) made him at once renowned. Although he has allowed his Jewish philosophy and his aversion to everything Christian to appear here and there, he has portrayed so well the life and customs of the people of the Black Forest, that a new interest in the life of the common people everywhere has been aroused. Later on were written his

FRITZ REUTER

long and well-known novels, which have a well-defined
political, democratic, or socialistic purpose. They are *Frau
Professorin, Auf der Höhe* (On the Height), *Das Landhaus
am Rhein* (Country House on the Rhine), and *Waldfried,*
which treats of the reconciliation between northern and
southern Germany during the years 1864-71. In the last
few years of his life he turned his attention to the village
tale once more, and among others wrote *Der Tolpatsch aus
Amerika* (Blockhead from America) and *Brigitta,* both of
which are among his best.

Among the comparatively few who have succeeded in
the humorous novel, FRITZ REUTER (1810-74) stands first,
although his works are written in the Platt-Deutsch dialect.
While passing through Berlin, he was arrested in 1833 for
some trifling misdemeanors of his student days in Jena.
For seven years he was dragged from one prison to another,
and although this treatment unfitted him for study, and put
an end to his legal career, it imbittered him so little that
he made these experiences the basis of *Ut mine Festungstid*
(My Prison Days). Having failed to accomplish anything
in the legal profession, he tried farming, but with no better
success. He became badly addicted to drink and the rest
of his life was one of wavering and incessant convivialities.
After his marriage his life became somewhat more settled,
and his wife was very influential in keeping him at his work
as a writer. *Ut de Franzosentid* (In the Year 1813) gives
a picture of the French occupation of Mecklenburg. *Ut
mine Stromtid* (My Farming Days) presents his farming
experiences, and will compare favorably with the best books
of humor in any language.

CHAPTER XVI.

RECENT AND CONTEMPORARY LITERATURE—Continued

DRAMATISTS.

The drama, like poetry and the novel, has felt the influence of political and social questions; but from its very nature it could not discuss these so fully as the novel. In the drama, too, more than in any other form of literature, German writers have been strongly influenced by foreign examples. Yet several men have won a very creditable place in dramatic production, and probably the most successful of these are GUTZKOW, LAUBE, LUDWIG, HEBBEL, FREYTAG, HEYSE, and WILDENBRUCH.

KARL GUTZKOW wrote quite a series of good pieces, which even to-day are popular with cultured audiences. *Uriel Acosta* depicts a noble-minded man's search for truth and his struggle between prejudice and freedom of thought. *Zopf und Schwert* (Cue and Sword) is a fine historical comedy, giving a good picture of Friedrich William I, of Prussia. For the celebration of Goethe's hundredth birthday, he wrote *Königslieutenant* (King's Lieutenant), in which he has dramatized an episode between young Goethe and Count Thorane.

HEINRICH LAUBE (1806-84) for a long time director of the Vienna theater, made his first great success in *Die Karlsschüler,* describing the school where Schiller was educated. This and his *Graf Essex* are still frequently put on the stage.

OTTO LUDWIG (1813-65) proved his dramatic talent with the tragedy *Der Erbförster,* the plot of which is a tragic conflict between a landowner and one of his employees who imagines that owing to his long service he can not be discharged. The story is repulsive, but holds the reader's attention from beginning to end. *Die Makabäer,* in which the deep religious life of the Jews is forcibly expressed, is more important and deeper. Ludwig has also written a large number of excellent stories, the best one being *Zwischen Himmel und Erde* (Between Heaven and Earth).

CHRISTIAN FRIEDRICH HEBBEL (1813-63) from very humble circumstances worked his way up to the rank of a learned man and important dramatist. His first important work was *Judith,* in which he treats the Jewish legend in a very sensational manner. Although this piece has many strong points, it is full of the horrible and repulsive. This same tendency appeared in his later works, especially in *Maria Magdalena,* and was probably the main reason why his works, notwithstanding their great poetical and dramatical qualties, have not maintained themselves on the stage. His greatest work is *Die Nibelungen,* in which he attempted to dramatize the old legends.

PAUL HEYSE has been most successful as a dramatist when he has remained free from foreign influences and avoided foreign subjects. His best are *Elizabeth Charlotte, Ludwig der Bayer, Hans Lange, Colberg,* and *Die Weiber von Schorndorf.*

ERNST VON WILDENBRUCH until very recently was regarded as Germany's strongest dramatist, but within the last few years dramatic criticism has changed, a new school has arisen, whose leaders rival Wildenbruch, and in the popular estimate, at least, surpass him. Yet in native dramatic genius he is their superior, and he more than any other author has followed the traditions of the classic period as embodied in Goethe and Schiller, and in this line has won extraordinary successes. He was born in Beyrott, in Syria, in 1845, and at the age of six went to Athens and then to Constantinople, where his father was German ambassador. Returning to Germany, he studied law, and finally entered the diplomatic service, in which he still holds a position.

After writing the two war epics *Vionville* (1874) and
Sedan (1875), Wildenbruch turned his attention to the
drama, and produced in rapid succession several pieces,
which remained either unnoticed or were severely criticised.
Die Quitzows (1888), however, won the hearts of his people
and established his renown. Chief among his dramas
previous to this are: *Karolinger,* which has for its background the dissolution of the empire under Louis the Pious;
Der Fürst von Verona (Prince of Verona) depicting the
strife between the Ghibellines and the Guelfs; and *Das
neue Gebot* (The New Decree), which carries the reader
into the stormy times of Emperor Henry IV and Pope
Gregory VII, and points out the evils arising from the celi-
bacy of the priesthood.

With *Die Quitzows* he began a series of Hohenzollern
dramas, in which he intended to represent dramatically the
chief events in Brandenburg history, and as Prussia became
the leading power in Germany, the development of her history becomes national in character. The first of this series
represents FRIEDRICH, the first of the Hohenzollern dynasty,
as he comes from his former home in South Germany to
his new territory, Brandenburg, and there attempts to establish law and order. The fated hero of the drama is DIETRICH
QUITZOW, a native nobleman who leads the opposition
against Friedrich. *Der Generalfeldoberst* (1889) has for
its background the early years of the Thirty Years' War,
and describes the almost hopeless condition of the young
Prussian state. These dramas were flattering to the whole
dynasty and to William II especially, but they were pro-
hibited in the royal theater. Although much discouraged
by this, the poet continued with a plan for a sequel to the
last-mentioned drama. This was *Der neue Herr* (The New
Ruler, 1891), and it represents the Great Elector in his
heroic efforts to raise prostrate Germany from the agonies
of the terrible war.

Heinrich und Heinrichs Geschlecht (King Henry, 1896), although not a Hohenzollern drama is patriotic in its nature. It portrays in clear and forcible manner the life of Henry IV, his unfortunate boyhood, his career as king and emperor, his long struggle with Pope Gregory VII, and his ignoble end. Although in this work Wildenbruch is strongly influenced by the realistic tendencies of his contemporaries, he has produced a drama of the older historical type, which may well be compared with the work of Schiller, Kleist, Hebbel, and Ludwig. This work won for its author the Schiller prize, which he had the good fortune to win once before. In his last dramatic production, *Willehalm* (1897), which was prepared for the celebration of the hundredth birthday of William I, the author returns to Hohenzollern subjects, and gives a legendary representation of some of those portions of Germany history which may be grouped about the great emperor.

CHAPTER XVII

PRESENT TENDENCIES

THE NATURALISTIC MOVEMENT.

National Development Germany has now been united for a quarter of a century; she has a strong central government, her scientific methods of investigation have become admired and imitated by the whole world, her commerce has risen to be comparable in importance to that of any other country, her industries and her products are established in every market; and all this has been accomplished largely since the war of 1870-71. Now energy is being directed toward the inner life, toward culture and refinement, and thus literature is once more becoming prominent in the struggle for social progress.

Present tendencies compared with the Storm and Stress Intellectual Germany of to-day resembles the intellectual Germany of a little more than a hundred years ago. Although the Storm and Stress agitation was composed of several separate and distinct movements, they all had the same purpose—to free the individual man from inherited restraints and lead him to his highest development. The kernel of the whole movement was revolt— revolt against the whole social and political organism. In German literature during the past few years the leading note has been revolt. A hundred years ago it was revolt of the middle classes against an aristocracy that had lost its better nature, now it is revolt of the working classes against the middle classes. Then it meant an upward movement in human development, and it is to be hoped that its meaning to-day is similar.

Foreign leaders As in the first Storm and Stress period the leaders were foreigners, so in the new period they are not Germans; then the great sources of inspiration were ROUSSEAU, DIDEROT, and RICHARDSON, now

From a Photograph by Gottheil & Sohn

HERMANN SUDERMANN

From a Photograph by F. Baruch

GERHART HAUPTMANN

they are IBSEN, ZOLA, and TOLSTOI.   But the similarity of
the movements is evident from the fact that now as well as
then German men of originality and power are taking the
place of these foreigners as leaders.   About the year 1890
the wild agitation and commotion of this new Storm and
Stress, the struggle between the realists and the idealists,
settled down into a conscious and well-defined naturalism.
This was contemporaneous with the appearance of several
talented men who at once won the public, while the movement had until then been largely confined to narrow circles.

From the large army of these naturalistic writers two
stand out more prominently than any others, and they may
be called the leaders.   They are SUDERMANN and HAUPT-
MANN.

HERMANN SUDERMANN (1857, now in Berlin) has known
how to take enough from the old and enough from the new
to please his audience and his readers, and of course this
means success.   Most of the successes of the naturalistic
school have been made in the drama, and although a large
number of novels have been written, Sudermann's are the
only ones that have even reached a second edition.   Sudermann himself believes that his great strength lies in the
direction of the novel and short story, but his works in general prove that his talent is equally strong in the drama.
Although his works are all tinged with the dark and melancholy side of life, his novels will compare favorably with
those of the great masters of all countries, who strive to
present real life in all its varying aspects and its complex-
ities and difficulties.   He has the gift of terse narration with
the simplest language, and a power for description that is
almost universal; terrible and heart-rending scenes and
joyful and pathetic or humorous situations are equally

Novels   within his grasp.   His great novels are *Frau
                    Sorge* (Dame Care, 1886), *Der Katzensteg* (Cat's
Bridge, 1888), and *Es War* (It Was, 1894).   The story of

the first centers in the sacrifices of a man who is born in the midst of financial difficulties, and whose brothers and sisters afterward owe their all to his unselfish devotion to duty. The heroine of the second is an uneducated child of nature who is endowed with native nobility and power of sacrifice. Sudermann is especially happy in his characterization of women, and this is nowhere better presented than in one of the leading characters of *Es War*. Hertha, in her simplicity and innocence, secretly loves a man older than herself, who is madly in love with the wife of his best friend.

Dramas In his dramas Sudermann would make the stage a teacher of morality by so presenting certain phases of life in all their ugliness and brutality, that his hearers must become sworn enemies of the evils he denounces. But his characters are apt to be contented with discussion and preaching, and they seem seldom called on to act. For this reason they frequently fail to reach the hearers' sympathy and thus fail in the best means of teaching. *Die Ehre* (Honor, 1889) is an exposure of numerous false ideas about honor and social conventions. *Sodom's Ende* (Sodom's End, 1891) has for its plot the artistic and physical collapse of a young painter on account of social influences that destroy all his nobleness of soul. *Heimat* (Home, better known as Magda, 1893) has for its theme parental and filial duty. It is the story of a talented girl leaving her home to win a place in the world as a singer, of her return in later years only to break her father's heart by once more disobeying him. *Morituri* (1896) is composed of three short pieces, each depicting a man conscious of approaching death. *Das Glück im Winkel* (Love in a Groove, 1896) presents the conflict based on that sin against nature which Goethe in *Die Wahlverwantschaften* so severely criticised; i. e., the marriage of a young and vigorous woman to an old man. *Johannes* (John the Baptist, 1897) marks a departure from the author's hitherto realistic and modern trend, and depicts the victory of Christian love over the heathen and Judaic world.

GERHART HAUPTMANN (1862, now in Berlin) with his *Vor Sonnenaufgang* (Before Sunrise, 1889) caused more commotion in Berlin and amid all classes than any previous work of the naturalistic school, and since then a series of dramas have appeared which have made him one of the foremost dramatists of Germany and of Europe. This first drama represents a family tragedy, and it is a terrible and forcible presentation of intemperance and its hereditary tendencies. Hell itself can not be worse than the misery here presented, and Zola and Ibsen might here learn to depict with cold-hearted brutality. *Die Weber* (Weavers, 1892) is the story of a strike, accompanied by tumult and riot, which is soon put down by military force. From beginning to end it is full of destruction and human misery, but the plot is developed with consummate skill and art. *Hannele* (1893), in which the delirious dream of a sick half-grown girl presents a vision of heaven, won over to the author a class of people who before had been repulsed by the suffering and misery in his works. They believed that he had turned from depicting hopeless victims to portraying the consolation of religion, but he who reads the drama carefully will see the cold, brutal picture of human suffering. In *Florien Geyer* (1895) the author turned to history for his material, and brings upon the stage scenes from the Peasants' War. The piece met with quite a fiasco when first presented, and although it has been remodeled and fairly successful, it can not be called equal to some of his earlier works. *Die versunkene Glocke* (The Sunken Bell, 1896) met with a most enthusiastic reception, and is generally regarded as one of his best if not his best work. The plot is based on the despair of a bell-founder, when his best work is destroyed. In the accident which destroys the bell, he is wounded, and his helpless condition appeals to a girl of the mountains, who wins him back to life, to labor, to happiness, but away from his home and family. Repentance leads him back home, only to find that his wife is no more. Returning to the mountains, he dies in the arms of his mountaineer companion. *Fuhrmann Henschel* (1898) marks another step in advance, and promises still greater things from the author.

Symbolism   In his other works Hauptmann has followed closely the principles of naturalism, but in the *Glocke,* something new is added. It is an almost indefinable, indescribable influence, which, since about 1893 or 1894, has been arising in opposition to naturalism. It is mystic or romantic in nature, and probably can best be referred to as the reaction against naturalism carried to the extreme. For the want of a better name, this has been called Symbolism. This movement is even now almost a thing of the past, and its only results are that it has taken much of the one-sidedness from naturalism, and left it a much stronger, sounder, and more artistic movement.

If we look back through the history of literature, we will see that there has been a change in literary principles whenever there have been changes of importance in philosophy or politics. Turning to the generation immediately preceding the fifties, we see that liberalism and realism made themselves felt as powers everywhere, while in the following generation liberalism gradually declined and placed capitalism in the ascendancy. Accompanying this movement there has been a decadence in literature. If now we search for the leading force in human striving, we will find the rising one to be something in the nature of Socialism, and the literary movement contemporary with this is Naturalism. Although Socialism and Naturalism both have their disagreeable, repulsive, and even terrible sides, may we not regard them as coexistent influences in different yet related fields exerting a powerful impulse in the upward march of mankind?

CHRONOLOGICAL TABLE.

223

About 1200 *Nibelungenlieb. Gudrun.*
Walther von der Vogel-
weide. Gottfried von
Strassburg. Hartmann von
Aue.

Magna Charta,	1215	
Crusades,	1091-1295	
Dante,	1265-1321	
University of Heidelberg,	1386	
Chaucer (1310-),	1400	Beginning of the Master-song.
University of Leipzig,	1409.	
Invention of printing,	1450	
	1483	Birth of Luther.
Discovery of America,	1492	
	1494	Brant's *Narrenschiff.*

NEW HIGH GERMAN LITERATURE.

1508 Luther called to Wittenberg.
1515 Till *Enlenspiegel.*
1517 Luther's Theses against Indulgences.

Diet of Worms, 1521
1523 Sachs's *'Wittenbergisch
Nachtigall.*
1534 Luther's Bible.
1546 Luther's Death.

University of Jena, 1558
Accession of Elizabeth,
Massacre of St. Bartholomew, **1572**
1575 Fischert's *Gargantua.*
1494-1576 Hans Sachs.
Fischert's *Glückhaft Schiff
von Zürich.*

Death of Mary Stuart, 1587 *Faustbuch.*
Montaigne, 1533-1592.
1602 *Der ewige Jude.*
Shakespeare, 1564-1616

Pilgrims in New England,   1620
                                        1624 O p i t z's *Buch von der*
                                             deutschen Poetrey.
Bacon,   1561-1626
French Academy,   1635
Harvard University,   1636
                               1597-1639 Opitz.
                               1609-1640 Paul Fleming.
Accession of Louis XIV,   1643
Thirty Years' War,   1618-1648
                               1604-1655 Friedrich von Logau.
                               1616-1664 Andreas Gryphius.
                                        1672 Weise's *Die drei ärgsten*
                                             Erznarren.
Molière,   1622-1673
Milton,   1608-1674
                               1618-1679 Hoffmannswaldau.
                               1635-1683 Lohenstein.
Corneille,   1606-1684
Bunyan,   1628-1688
Racine,   1639-1699
Dryden,   1631-1700
Yale University,
Death of Louis XIV,   1715
                                  1721 Leipzig-Swiss Controversy.
                                       Discourse der Malern.
                                  1729 Birth of Lessing.
                                  1732 Bodmer's Milton's *Paradise*
                                       Lost.
University of Göttingen,   1733
                                  1739 The Anacreontics.
Alexander Pope (1688-),   1744 *Bremer Beiträge.*
                                  1746 Gellert's *Fabeln und Erzäh-*
                                       lungen.
                                  1748 Klopstock's *Messias.* Les-
                                       sing's *Der junge Gelehrte.*
                                  1749 Birth of Goethe.
                                  1758 Gleim's *Preussische Kriegs-*
                                       lieder.
                                  1759 Lessing's *Litteraturbriefe.*

15

Seven Years' War in Ger-
many,   1756-1763

1764 Winkelmann's *Geschichte
der Kunst des Altertums.*

Stamp Act Congress,   1765 Goethe at Leipzig.

1766 Lessing's *Laokoon.*
Wieland's Shakespeare.

1767 Lessing's' *Minna von Barnhelm* and *Hamburgische
Dramaturgie.*

1770 Goethe and Herder in
Strassburg.

1771 Claudias's *Wansbecker Bote.*

First Partition of Poland,   1772 Lessing"s *Emilia Galotti.*
The Göttingen Hainbund.
Wieland in Weimar.

Boston Tea Party,   1773 Goethe's *Götz von Berlich-
ingen.*
Bürger's *Lenore.* *Messias*
completed.
Schiller at the Karlsschule.

Goldsmith,   1728-1774

Beginning of Karl Au-
gust's reign,   1775 Goethe at Weimar.

Battle of Bunker Hill,

Declaration of Independence,   1776 Klinger's *Sturm und Drang.*

Battle of Saratoga,   1777

Voltaire (1694-),   1778 Herder's *Volkslieder.*

Rousseau (1712-),

1779 Lessing's *Nathan der Weise.*

1780 Wieland's *Oberon.*

American Confederation,   1781 Death of Lessing. Schiller's
Die Räuber.

1782 Schiller's Flight from
Stuttgart.

Peace of Versailles,   1783 Schiller's *Fiesco.* Schiller
at Bauerbach. Voss's
Luise.

	1784	Herder's *Ideen zur Philosophie der Geschichte der Menschheit.*
		Schiller's *Kabale und Liebe.*
	1785	Schiller in Leipzig.
Death of Frederick the Great,	1786	Goethe in Italy (-1788) Writing *Iphigenie, E g m o n t, Torquato Tasso.*
Philadelphia Convention,	1787	Schiller in Weimar. *Don Carlos.*
		Goethe's *Iphigenie.*
	1788	Schiller in Volkstedt. *Abfall der Niederlande.*
		Goethe's *Egmont.*
Beginning of the French Revolution,	1789	Schiller Professor at Jena. *Die Künstler.*
		Goethe's *Torquato Tasso.*
Franklin (1706-),	1790	Jean Paul's *Schulmeisterlein Wuz.*
	1793	Schiller's Visit to Swabia. Jean Paul's *Unsichtbare Loge.*
French Reign of Terror (1793-),	1794	Goethe and Schiller United.
	1795	Goethe's *Wilhelm Meisters Lehrjahre. Die Horen.* Jean Paul's *Hesperus.*
Robert Burns (1759),	1796	*Xenien.* Jean Paul's *Quintus Fixlein. Musenalmanach.*
Burke (1729-),	1797	*Ballaaenalmandch.* Goethe's *Hermann und Dorothea* Schlegel's Shakespeare. Schiller's Ballad Year.
	1798	Schlegel's *Athenäum.* Tieck's *Franz Sternbald.*
Napoleon Made Consul,	1799	Schiller's *Wallenstein.* Removal to Weimar. Fr. Schlegel's *Lucinde.*

	1800 Schiller's *Maria Stuart, Das Lied von der Glocke.* Jean Paul's *Titan.*
	1801 Schiller's *Jungfrau von Orleans.*
Purchase of Louisiana,	1803 Schiller's *Braut von Messina.* Death of Klopstock, Herder, and Gleim.
Napoleon Crowned Emperor,	1804 Schiller's *Wi.helm Tell.* Jean Paul's *Flegeljahre.*
	1805 Schiller's Death. Publication of Herder's *Cid.* Arndt's *Geist der Zeit.*
Battle of Jena,	1806 Arnim and Brenatno's *Des Knaben Wunderhorn.*
	1808 Goethe's *Faust,* Part I.
	1809 Goethe's *Wahlverwantschaften.*
University of Berlin,	1810 Kleist's *Kätchen von Heilbronn.*
	1811 Goethe's *Dichtung und Wahrheit.* Fouqués *Undine.* Kleist's *Der zerbrochene Krug.*
Napoleon's Russian Campaign, English-American War, Battle of Leipzig,	1812 Körner's *Zriny.*
	1813 Arndt's *Lieder für Deutsche.* Death of Wieland and Körner.
	1814 Körner's *Leier und Schwert.* Rüdkert's *Deutsche Gedichte.* Chamisso's *Schlemihl.*
Congress of Vienna, Battle of Waterloo,	1815 Uhland's Poems. Schenkendorf's Poems. Fr. Schlegel's *Geschichte der alten und neuen Litteratur.*

	1817	Grillparzer's *Ahnfrau.*
		Death of Schenkendorf.
University of Bonn,	1818	Uhland's *Ernst, Herzog, von Schwaben.*
		Grillparzer's *Sappho.*
	1819	Goethe's *W e s t - Östlicher Dirvan.*
Shelley (1792-),	1822	Rückert's *Liebesfrühling.*
		Heine's Poems.
		Uhland's *Walther von der Vogelweide.*
Byron,	1788-1824	
	1825	Death of Jean Paul.
	1826	Eichendorf's *Taugenichts.*
		Hauff's *Lichtenstein.*
		Death of Voss.
		Heine's *Harzreise.*
	1827	Heine's *Buch der Lieder.*
Karl August's Rule,	1775-1828	
Jackson, President,	1829	Goethe's *Wilhelm Meisters Wanderjahre.*
		Chamisso's *Salas y Gomez.*
Louis Philippe, King of France,	1830	Grün's *Der letzte Ritter.*
Walter Scott (1771-),	1832	Death of Goethe. *Faust,* Part II.
Coleridge,	1772-1834.	
Coronation of Victoria,	1837	Halm's *Grisildis.*
		Lenau's *Savanarola.*
	1843	Auerbach's *Schwarzwälder Darfgeschichten.*
	1846	Kinkel's *Otto der Schütz.*
		Gutzkow's *Uriel Akosta.*
		Heine's *Atta Troll.*
Gold in California,	1848	Freiligrath and Kinkel, Political Refugees.
Revolutions in Germany and France and the Second Republic,		

Frankfort Parliament, Poe (1809-),	1849 Redwitz's *Amaranth*.
Wordsworth (1770-),	1850 Storm's *Immensee*.
Cooper (1789-),	1851 Roquette's *Waldmei s t e r s Brautfahrt*.
	Heine's *Romancero*.
Second Empire in France,	1852
	1854 Scheffel's *Trompeter v o n Säkkingen*.
	Freytag's *Die Journalisten*.
	Ludwig's *Die Makkabäer*.
	Halm's *Fechter von Ravenna*.
	1855 Freytag's *Soll und Haben*.
	1799-1856 Heine.
	Laube's *Graf Essex*.
Crimean War (1854-),	Freiligrath's Longfellow's *Hiawatha*.
	1857 Scheffel's *Ekkehard*.
	Geibel's *Brunhild*.
	1860 Spielhagen's *Problematische Naturen*.
	Death of Arndt.
Lincoln, President,	1861
	1862 Death of Uhland and Kerner.
	Hebbel's *Die Nibelungen*.
Hawthorne (1804-),	1864 Ebers's *Eine ägyptische Königstochter*.
Civil War,	1861-1865
Austrian-Prussian War,	1866 Freytag's *Verlorene Handschrift*.
	Reuter's *Utmine Stromtid*.
	Death of *Rüchert*.
	1867 Scheffel's *Guadeamus*.
Grant, President,	1869 Geibel's *Sophonisbe* wins Schiller Prize.
Dickens (1812-),	1870 Freiligrath's *Hurra Germania,* and *Die Trompete von Gravelotte*.

Franco-German War,	1870-1871 Death of Halm and Alexis.
	1873 Heyse's *Kinder der Welt*.
	1874 Jordon's *Nibelunge*.
	Auerbach's *Walfried*.
Centennial Celebration,	1876 Dahn's *Kampf um Rom*.
	1877 Spielhagen's *Sturmflut*.
	1878 Weber's *Dreizenlinden*.
	Fontane's *Vor dem Sturm*.
	1880 Wolff's *Tannhäuser*.
Assassination of Garfield,	1881 Ebers's *Frau Bürgermeist-erin*.
	Baumbach's *Frau Holde*.
Emerson (1803),	1882 Death of Kinkel and Auer-
Longfellow (1807),	bach.
	1815-1884 Geibel.
Victor Hugo,	1802-1885
	1886 Wolff's *Lorelei*.
	Heyse's *Der Roman der Stiftdame*.
	Sudermann's *Frau Sorge*.
Louisa M. Alcott (1832-),	1888 Wildenbruch's *Die Quit-zows*.
Mathew Arnold (1822-),	Sudermann's *Der Katzen-steg*.
Browning (1812-),	1889 Hauptmann's *Vor Sonnen-aufgang*.
	Sudermann's *Die Ehre*.
	Wildenbruch's *Der General-feldoberst*.
Retirement of Bismarck,	1890 Death of Keller.
Lowell (1819-),	1891 Wolff's *Renata*.
	Sudermann's *Sodom's Ende*.
	Wildenbruch's *Der neue Herr*.
Whittier (1807-),	1892 Weber's *Goliath*.
Tennyson (1809)	Wolff's *Der fliegende Hol-lender*.
	Heyse's *Merlin*.
	Hauptmann's *Die Weber*.

Columbian Exposition,	1893	Eber's *Cleopatra.*
		Wildenbruch's *E i f e r n d e Liebe.*
		Spielhagen's *Sonntagskind.*
		Sudermann's *Heimat.*
		Hauptmann's *Hannele.*
Oliver W. Holmes (1809),	1894	Ebers's *Im Schmiedefeuer.*
		Wildenbruch's *Schwester- seele.*
		Sudermann's *Es War.*
	895	Ebers's *Im blauen Hecht.*
		Heyse's *Ueber allen Gipfeln.*
		Spielhagen's *Susi.*
		Dahn's *Chlodovech.*
		Hauptmann's *F l o r i a n Geyer.*
William Morris (1834-),	1896	Ebers's *Barbara Blomberg.*
		Wildenbruch's *Heinrich und Heinrichs Geschlecht.*
		Sudermann's *Das Glück im Winkel.*
		Hauptmann's *Die versun- kene Glocke.*
		Wolff's *Assalide.*
		Heyse's *Abenteuer eines Blaustrümpfchens.*
		Spielhagen's *Selbstgereht.*
	1897	Ebers's *Arachne.*
		Dahn's *Ebroin.*
		Wildenbruch's *Willehalm Tiefe Wasser.*
		Sudermann's *Johannes.*
Spanish-American War,	1898	Hauptmann's *Fuhrmann Henschel.*
		Death of Ebers.

INDEX.

Numbers refer to pages. Titles are printed in italics.